LEAN
TO
THE
CORPS

A First-Hand Account of the U.S. Marine Corps'

– Lean Six Sigma Journey –

Plus STREAMLINED LEAN SIX SIGMA for EVERYONE

Susan L. Stuffle, P.E.

For Kim, who has been by my side for much of this journey – you are the best!
And for the three most important men in my life: Doug, Nathan, and Caleb.

A bit of history… a bit of how-to… and a bit of humor. I hope you will not only enjoy this book, but will consider ways that you can use the approach and lessons detailed herein to benefit your life and loved ones.

Table of Contents

Table of Figures:

Lean to the Corps

EVERYTHING we do is a process… every process can be improved.

Preface

What is Lean Six Sigma?

Quantico, Virginia: "… sounds like a fraternity". That was the initial response I received from one of the first Marine Corps General Officers who agreed to meet with me on the topic of Lean Six Sigma. I will never forget that meeting. I was nervous, younger, and found myself sitting on the visitor (subservient) side of a massive desk, across from a revered Marine Corps General. I recall his office, located at the end of a red and blue carpeted hallway. The walls were lined with United States Marine Corps historical photographs, exuding an aura that made even a 30-something woman (like me, at the time) want to find the nearest recruiter to say "sign me up!"

Those were the early days of carrying the water around Marine Corps Headquarters, explaining the strange-sounding term. That response has stayed with me, and has reminded me that the term Lean Six Sigma, while so engrained and familiar – positive and proven in my mind, does sound like a fraternity to those who have never been trained or have yet to see the results of this fantastic approach to process improvement.

What is Lean Six Sigma? I get that question a lot. I also receive many retorts such as "we don't need this", "we already do this", or "this will come and go, just like everything else". I never let these comments deter me. Because I know from experience that down the road the very people who were initially negative, or unenthusiastic at the least, will most likely utter comments such as "I wish I had done this sooner" or "I see everything differently now".

I have been blessed with a very good life. I have a family I love and have spent many years at a job that I love: working side-by-side with America's Finest, United States Marines of all ages and ranks, to help them find ways to conduct their work more efficiently, supporting each other to the best of their abilities. These honorable, smart, strong men and women risk their lives so that you and I (and countless others around the world) can enjoy freedom and a better quality of life. I ask you, what better job can there be than helping Marines?

At any rate, back to the question: What is Lean Six Sigma?

Lean Six Sigma, or LSS, is an integration of two process improvement methodologies: Lean and Six Sigma. When these methodologies are applied to any process, the resulting process is improved, usually in the areas of cost, quality, and/or timeliness. This means that the new process may be faster, cheaper, or more reliable.

To further explain, let's get down to basics. Think about anything you do… at home, work, or anywhere. What you do is a "process". It has a beginning step, middle steps, and a final step – all of these steps combine to produce some sort of outcome. For example, you may travel to the store, buy groceries, and return home on a regular basis, which results in having food in your house; manufacturers gather parts and conduct production steps resulting in a car, or a pair of shoes, or, you name it; a college student attends class, studies, and takes an exam, resulting in a grade and ultimately a degree. One of my favorite sayings is this: EVERYTHING we do is a process, every process can be improved.

We use "Lean" tools to review processes, looking for what is called "waste". Waste is anything above and beyond what is absolutely necessary to create a desired outcome. The desired outcome is often called a "product" or "service". "Six Sigma" tools are used to review processes, looking for ways to reduce problems, often called "defects". Six Sigma also emphasizes standardization, ensuring that the best way to conduct the steps of a process is documented and followed. So, a "Lean Six Sigma" process is conducted as quickly as possible, using the fewest resources necessary, and performed the same way regardless of who is participating in the process. Waste, variation, and defects are all minimized.

The history of these tools, along with further technical descriptions, can be found in countless books. A simple internet search will reveal thousands of hits on the topic. Also, some of my favorite publications on Lean Six Sigma (and more) are listed in a recommended reading section at the end of this book.

The good news is that <u>every single one of us is ALREADY a process improvement expert</u>. This is true particularly when we have complete control of the situation and are personally affected. Consider getting to work every day: Do you take the longest route possible?

Lean to the Corps

When you first started traveling your current route to work, did you try a few alternatives and then select the most efficient route? Of course! We all do that. Even if there are constraints, such as transporting children to school at a certain time, we will still find the most efficient way to get to work while addressing the constraint. Congratulations, you are already a process improvement expert!

PART 1. A BIT OF HISTORY:
THE BEGINNING

– "It's like diving into common sense."
Lean Six Sigma Green Belt Student, November 2009, Marine
Corps Air Station Miramar

The Vision

Colonel (Retired) Dave Clifton is a man of vision, carrying the weight of the world on his shoulders because of it. He predicted the housing bubble, and talks of the "fiscal tsunami" in our future if the United States doesn't change course. He follows publications of the likes of David Walker[1]... and has a jarring ability to see through the haze of the unknown future to lock onto specific items of concern. He then proceeds to share his concerns with those of us who otherwise would remain peacefully oblivious. It has been a few years since the two of us sat down to one of these informative discussions over lunch, but I have no doubt that if we crossed paths today, he would have details to share regarding the next thing for which to be prepared. And, I would leave the discussion with a heightened sense of concern combined with a determination to be ready, which I think is his aim.

Given this personality, it's probably not surprising that Colonel Clifton has spent the past couple of decades looking for tools to help the U.S. Marine Corps better manage finances and resources. As a Financial Management Officer, he began influencing Marine Corps fiscal approaches while serving as Comptroller at Marine Corps Forces, Pacific (MARFORPAC), in Hawaii. During his next and final active-duty assignment, while located in the Navy Annex of the Pentagon, he guided the Marine Corps' sprint toward Lean Six Sigma, after a marathon of useful and well-intentioned predecessors. This final sprint

---

[1] David Walker, former Comptroller General for U.S. Government Accountability Office (1998-2008)

included institutionalizing Activity Based Costing (ABC)[2] and establishing Business Performance Offices at each of 27 world-wide installations, to better understand the total costs associated with the primary activities of the Marine Corps. ABC was a good stepping stone toward continuous process improvement, as was the dabble in ISO-9000, Malcolm Baldrige, and other known process and analysis tools for organizations. For a variety of reasons, these tools came and went (I would be remiss not to mention that there may be organizations within the Marine Corps who still use these tools).

After years of searching spurred by a natural inclination to seek improvement, Colonel Clifton crossed paths with a gentleman named Don Esmond. Mr. Esmond, the Senior Vice President for Automotive Operations at Toyota Motor Sales U.S.A, was also a retired Marine. In the summer of 2004, Mr. Esmond was an honored guest at a Marine Corps Sunset Parade, held at the foot of the Iwo Jima Memorial, surrounded by the "President's Own" U.S. Marine Band and the Silent Drill Team. A friendly discussion that evening resulted in a visit by Colonel Clifton to the University of Toyota, located in Torrance, CA. Toyota America sends new employees to the University for an introduction to the culture of continuous process improvement, also known in Toyota circles as "Kaizen". Through some hands-on exercises that involved toy cars - of course! - (with a tongue-in-cheek comparison of Toyota's just-in-time processing and other manufacturer's inventory heavy processing), Colonel Clifton was himself introduced to the Toyota culture of not only continuous process improvement, but also thoughtful humility, benevolence, and family. He immediately saw a connection with the Marine Corps.

Looking toward the Marine Corps' fiscal future, he was able to lock onto Toyota's ideology, and a vision was born. In hindsight, for the rest of us, this was a perfectly logical direction. But, without the benefit of hindsight, it took a special insight to recognize: The Marine Corps' culture of Honor, Courage, Commitment plus austere environment and most certain budget shortfalls in the future would

---

[2] Activity Based Costing (ABC) is a methodology used to identify total costs (including both direct and indirect costs) associated with individual activities of an organization. Traditional accounting tends to categorize costs without assessing costs by activity.

benefit greatly by pursuing continuous process improvement using the Toyota model[3] (which I will refer to as "Lean" in this book).

The natural pairing of Lean and Six Sigma then became our pursuit. Establishing lean processes and standardizing those practices across the Marine Corps was our goal. While this would logically result in reduced resource needs (dollars, people, supplies) for these processes, our emphasis from day one has been IMPROVED SUPPORT FOR THE WARFIGHTER.

Flavor of the Month: So Many Alternatives for Process Improvement

In this day of self-improvement, business improvement, life improvement, health improvement, and fill-in-the-blank improvement, you can't swing a dead idea without hitting a book on the topic. Don't get me wrong, I'm all about looking at things and figuring out how to make them better. The problem is that if you follow too many good ideas, you may miss out on the great ones[4]. It's easy to get lost in a cloud of worthwhile tools and effort. But once you begin the Lean Six Sigma journey, everything else pales in comparison. Allowing a Lean Six Sigma program to grab hold and mature in your organization (by the way, the approach described in this book is completely scalable – it applies to huge enterprises such a Motorola, Toyota, General Electric as well as the local family owned restaurant or home-based business) is the best gift you can ever give yourself, and consequently the best gift your organization can give to others who benefit from the products or services you produce. Don't fall into the temptation of diluting your Lean Six Sigma approach with other good ideas. If you keep a laser focus, using the approach described in this book, you WILL see your processes improve.

In my twenty-plus years working as an industrial engineer with the Department of Defense (Navy prior to Marine Corps), I've lived

---

[3] Toyota Production System (TPS) encourages finding ways to reduce waste and become more efficient in every process associated with production. A generic term for this approach is known as "Lean". Lean is used by many organizations, with Toyota being one of the best known and best at employing the practice.

[4] See Collins, chapter 1, for an excellent explanation of this concept. Collins, Jim. *Good to Great*. New York: HarperCollins, 2001. Print.

through many of the flavors of the month: Quality Circles, Tiger Teams, Total Quality Management, Total Quality Leadership – all with good intentions, and honestly, good tools. I prefer to think of these process improvement attempts as the predecessors to Lean Six Sigma. Much like a computer: recall computers from decades ago. Remember the large and heavy monitors, complete with black screen and either green or orange letters glowing with that background of nothingness? Funny now, but they served a purpose. Without those computers, we wouldn't have the electronic age of today with laptops, tablets, a smart phone in every hand, some on wrists. Our flavors of the month served their purpose, leading us to this advanced approach to process improvement called Lean Six Sigma. The difference now is that with Lean Six Sigma there is not a need to move on to another approach, but rather to just get better at implementing it until it becomes a part of our culture (as we have seen with Toyota).

Marine Corps Martial Arts Program

Once the Marine Corps decided to embrace Lean Six Sigma[5], the detailed planning began. One key decision had to do with the Marine Corps Martial Arts Program, MCMAP. In the Lean Six Sigma world, levels of knowledge and capability are described as "belt colors", much like in martial arts programs.

Officially, these terms are used:

LSS BELT COLOR	TRAINING REQUIREMENT	ROLES/RESPONSIBILITIES
Green Belt	40 hours	Lead smaller scoped projects Train team members Hold key role in larger scoped projects Possibly coach and mentor other Green Belts

---

[5] It should be noted, Marine Corps Aviation adopted LSS prior to the rest of the Marine Corps as a part of the Naval Aviation Enterprise program. The Aviation approach differed a bit from the non-Aviation community; but there was a continuing effort to standardize LSS across the entire Marine Corps.

Black Belt	Green Belt + 160 hours	Green Belt responsibilities + Lead larger scoped projects Train Green Belts Coach and mentor others
Master Black Belt	Black Belt + Years of Experience	Black Belt responsibilities + Train Black Belts Certify Green and Black Belts Initiate and manage LSS programs Develop templates, documents, and training materials

Figure 1 LSS "Belt" Color Progression

Unofficially, additional terms are used:

LSS BELT COLOR	TRAINING REQUIREMENT	PURPOSE/ROLES/RESPON SIBILITIES
White Belt	1-2 hours	Basic Introduction to Lean Six Sigma Principles, which is useful for: Anyone in general Potential Green/Black Belts Leadership and Stakeholders
Yellow Belt	8-16 hours	Introduction to Lean Six Sigma Principles (with exercises), which is useful for: Project team members Potential Green/Black Belts Leadership and Stakeholders

Figure 2 LSS Unofficial "Belt" Colors

This belt color terminology is standard for Lean Six Sigma in the private sector. However, those of us who were planning the Marine Corps' Lean Six Sigma program approached these terms with trepidation. After all, MCMAP is a sacred thing for Marines. It takes serious time, skill, and effort to earn the MCMAP belts. If our terminology was offensive to Marines, we could fail before we even began.

During initial planning, we considered alternate terms: Level 1, Level 2, and Level 3 in place of Green Belt, Black Belt, and Master Black Belt. But, after much consideration and a bit of debate, it was settled. We would stick with the martial arts sounding terms. The deciding factor was this: if Marines were to train and become experts in Lean Six Sigma at Levels 1, 2, and 3, that would not transfer smoothly to the private sector. Therefore, a Marine with LSS skills would not easily be able to translate those skills to a resume and potential job opportunity once his or her service came to a conclusion. By trying to not offend Marines, replacing the martial arts references in LSS with alternatives, we would actually hurt their future job prospects. Using that perspective, the right decision became obvious: adopt the belt color terminology to align with industry.

Early Interactions with Toyota

Interactions with Toyota North America expanded to include site visits by Marines (and civilians) to manufacturing plants, distribution centers, and the University of Toyota. This occurred during the period when we were learning about Lean Six Sigma, and how it might be a good fit for the Marine Corps.

Timing could not have been better. Like a perfect storm, the lessons learned in the Toyota Lean Thinking training ignited a level of energy with our Director, followed by the rest of our small team of engineers and analysts. We began to envision the culture of continuous improvement that would come with formally introducing Lean Six Sigma to Marines. At this point I should state that the Marine Corps embodies and always has had a culture of continuous improvement –

they are America's First to Fight[6] force. With about eight percent of the entire Department of Defense budget[7], they get the job done. No matter what. No better friend, no worse enemy than the United States Marine!

That said, and truly the case, there is ALWAYS room for improvement. Remember, every process can be improved.

Our team began to discuss the possibilities. We assessed how to train and support Marines, how to gain support of leadership, where to begin, and what guidance to develop. We even developed a logo[8] and ordered matching shirts with that logo embroidered on the left chest. We branded ourselves as the Marine Corps' internal consultants for Lean Six Sigma. While big wins would be good, we would be thrilled to help Marines experience smaller continuous improvements that would eventually result in large benefits. – This discussion reminds me of a poster that I saw on the wall at the University of Toyota: it contained hundreds of small pebbles with a caption that described continuous improvement through an explanation of "Kaizen". The gist was that by combining many smaller efforts and efficiencies, the results can be exciting and significant.

Over the next few years, our team was to visit the University of Toyota on two occasions. The first was to attend the practitioner training mentioned earlier. During the second visit, we were honored to hold question and answer sessions with instructors, leaders, and employees. These were enlightening in that both Toyota and the Marine Corps faced many of the same struggles with continuous improvement.

Toyota's culture is not only one of continuous pursuit of perfection, but also of benevolence. Toyota leadership considered these hosting opportunities as a sort of public service. They hosted many visitors in addition to Marines, including competing auto manufacturers! During our interactions, this was described as an opportunity to serve others. We returned from these visits invigorated, with renewed senses of determination and direction.

---

[6] A collection of "First to Fight" accounts were published by Lieutenant General (Ret) Victor Krulak. Krulak, Victor. *First to Fight*. Annapolis, MD: Naval Institute Press, 1984. Print.

[7] Source: Commandant of the Marine Corps 2014 Report to Congress on the Posture of the United States Marine Corps, March 12, 2014

[8] The logo and team name consisted of three letters: CPI (which stands for Continuous Process Improvement) and a tag line "Performance Excellence".

Lean to the Corps

In April of 2008 we were given the honor of reciprocation. We were able to host a visit to Quantico, Virginia, by Toyota North America leaders from both the Toyota and Lexus lines. What topic interested them most regarding our Marine Corps? Would you like to take a guess? That's right – LEADERSHIP. The Toyota visitors spent time with the Director of the Marine Corps University[9] and Leaders at The Basic School[10]. They visited the Marine Corps Museum, and Officer Candidate School[11]. During down times we continued to discuss Toyota culture and practices, helping to solidify the approach we were to take with Marines.

These early interactions with Toyota, between 2005 and 2008, were a key ingredient of the mixture that would make up the concrete foundation of our Lean Six Sigma program.

It's a Go

In 2005, the Marine Corps Business Enterprise office was given approval to pursue Lean Six Sigma. This involved hiring a cadre of LSS Black Belts, Master Black Belts, and training a few of the existing engineers and analysts already on hand. The Marine Corps version of "cadre" was 15-20 people. Following the Marine Corps way, this small group of people were to support training and projects across bases and installations world-wide. By 2006, initial hiring and contracts were settled, all of the "plank-owners"[12] were on board.

We put out an order from Headquarters introducing the concept of Lean Six Sigma to the Marine Corps, with an initial focus on engaging at the base and installation level. The "business office" at each installation was asked to meet with local leadership to identify areas

---

[9] Marine Corps University, located at Marine Corps Base Quantico Virginia, trains and prepares leaders through professional military education and training.

[10] The Basic School, located at Marine Corps Base Quantico Virginia, trains newly commissioned or appointed officers.

[11] Officer Candidate School, located at Marine Corps Base Quantico Virginia, trains officer candidates prior to commissioning as Marine Corps officers.

[12] The designation of "plank-owner" is held with pride by those who receive it. It is a Naval tradition to bestow this title to an individual who was a member of the first crew of a ship at the time of commissioning. For more information see www.history.navy.mil.

ripe for improvement. The people who worked in those areas would then be trained to participate as team members to help improve their own areas. Support would be provided by local business staff, partnering with the Headquarters LSS representative assigned to help. This approach was met with enthusiasm by some installation members, negativity by some, and indifference by others. This combination of responses became the standard we received at any level of engagement. So true, regardless of whether I was interacting with young Marines, experienced Gunnery Sergeants and Master Sergeants, or Full-Bird Colonels and General Officers. The way I looked at it, there were not enough of us in our small cadre of LSS missionaries to pursue those who weren't interested in Lean Six Sigma. We would start with those who welcomed us, and hope that our good results would serve as proof of concept for those who were initially reluctant. It's probably obvious, but I will also mention that some Marines are somewhat scary – you know, the no nonsense types who growl in place of speaking. They may naturally be this way, or the years of placing themselves in harm's way and responding to our nation's call (often these days with no knowledge by the general public) has rightfully calloused their personalities. These scary Marines are the hardest to win over, but once they do approve of Lean Six Sigma (or anything), they are major influencers. There are few things as satisfying as gaining the trust of this type of Marine.

Perhaps it's time for a brief lesson on how the Marine Corps is organized, for those of you who have not had interactions with the military (like me, during the first 22 years of my life). This may be an oversimplification, so please accept my apology if you are a military expert and feel that this description doesn't meet muster (I threw that term in on purpose, with hopes that you will enjoy it and forgive me)[13]. In the "National Capitol Region (NCR)" where the Pentagon (Headquarters) is located, there are agencies and commands that help run the Marine Corps. The majority of these are located at the Pentagon or Marine Corps Base, Quantico Virginia. These organizations are in charge of important requirements, such as training, manpower, acquisition, logistics (not at Quantico), etc. Beyond the NCR, there are installations, or bases, located world-wide. These bases have varying missions, but in general they each have supporting staff who are

---

[13] Please note that for the most part Marine Corps Aviation is not included in this description.

assigned directly to the installation, also known as installation personnel. The NCR organizations and global installation personnel were the focus of our initial Lean Six Sigma efforts. However, each base, in addition to employing support personnel, also is home to the operators and tenants. These are the Marines (and some Navy – we appreciate your service, too!) who conduct the exercises, training and preparations to make sure our world's premier fighting force is always ready to go. For the sake of simplicity, I will call these Marines the "warfighters". While warfighters work and often live on the installations when not deployed, they were not asked to participate in Lean Six Sigma. At least not initially. The funny thing is, here we are many years later – Lean Six Sigma has proven to not be a "flavor of the month." We have improved countless processes, saved lots of money, improved readiness, and helped create conditions for a better quality of work life for many. Demand is not declining, nor is it steady – but rather, it continues to grow! Training and support requests arrive every day. Would you like to guess who is making the majority of these requests? … the WARFIGHTERS! They have never been directed or asked to participate in Lean Six Sigma, but they are seeking it anyhow. I believe this phenomenon is due to two factors: (1) word of mouth about results has been the best marketer for Lean Six Sigma, and (2) the Marines recognize this is a life-long skill that will benefit them and serve as a credential well after they conclude their work for the Corps.

A few years into the Marine Corps' Lean Six Sigma journey, we reached a perpetual state: proven results generating further interest and demand, generating more proven results. At this point, borrowing from Abraham Lincoln, the Lean Six Sigma program would "live forever, or die by suicide."

PART 2. A BIT OF HISTORY: PERFECT FIT

– "The Marine Corps is not a business. The Marine Corps is a combat force… these performance improvement tools are designed to support the Marine Corps' warfighter."
Colonel (Ret) Dave Clifton, August 2009, MCAGCC 29 Palms

Honor, Courage, and Commitment
+ Optimism, Humility, and Wisdom

Honor, Courage, and Commitment are the core values held by every Marine. These values guide Marines as they successfully transform in boot camp from a civilian to a member of the elite fighting force. These values continue to guide Marines through times of war, peace, strength, pain, joy… life. They are steeped in tradition and honor.

A few Sundays ago, the sermon at my church was about Daniel. Our Pastor described Daniel as a man with optimism, humility, and wisdom. He had been stolen away from his family at a young age, worked his way up in a foreign land and gained notice of a King. He refused to turn from what he knew was right, and ultimately influenced many in his time and for centuries after. After all, here we are, in the 21st century, talking about Daniel in a book about the Marine Corps and Lean Six Sigma!

I was struck by these characteristics: optimism, humility, and wisdom. These are the qualities I strive to have and convey as I support Marines and help improve processes. They fit, like the perfect puzzle piece, right up next to the ethos of Marines: Honor, Courage, and Commitment. If a man or woman has dedicated himself or herself to live a life of honor and courageously commit that life (even to the death) to serve our country, then I owe it to him or her to provide my brand of help, minuscule as it is in comparison, with optimism, humility, and wisdom.

Lean to the Corps

Why optimism? Without putting on glasses that are too rose-colored, it's necessary to enter any situation believing something positive will result. Optimism expresses itself in many ways: in addition to words that naturally come to mind and tone of voice, people can see it in your posture, sparkle and sincerity of eye contact. Process improvement may initially seem a bit soft and fuzzy to the recipient of the message. More so, when addressing a Marine. Talk about a tough audience! First responses are often negative, or uninterested at the least – "…sounds like a fraternity." I'll never forget that one. But, if you believe you are bringing something to people that will truly help them, not just in the immediate future, but for the rest of their lives, then you can't help but feel optimism! It's your job to convince the horse to drink the water.

Why humility? Arrogance is not appreciated in any environment. It is a show-stopper in the Marine Corps. It is cause to be quickly ushered to the exit if you are an arrogant civilian addressing Marines. While outwardly curtly smiling and nodding, they are very polite after all, Marines have no tolerance for arrogance. Trouble can arise if the wrong people are hired to support Lean Six Sigma. LSS Black Belts and Master Black Belts come with a lot of education, and are often the most mathematically talented people in the room. Some have perhaps been known to hold such statistically intensive conversations that a normal human's eyes glaze over, which might be mistaken for awe by a non-humble deliverer. As touted by Jim Collins[14], there are many people with great degrees and credentials, but unless the right people are brought "on the bus", or hired, trouble will ensue. So, humility is a necessary characteristic. Shame on the Lean Six Sigma expert who is so enamored with himself or herself that the audience is lost even before getting started. I've seen this happen, and it is not pretty. Plus, it poisons the well for others who may come later to offer help to Marines. Totally unacceptable.

Why Wisdom? I have a wonderful mentor. I can approach him with any question and he will have a personal story to share that clearly provides an answer. While I have had a number of great Lean Six Sigma experiences, my mentor has had 20 more years of experience and seven more published books. He is wise, and kind (and the

---

[14] See Collins, chapter 3. Collins, Jim. *Good to Great*. New York: HarperCollins, 2001. Print.

antithesis of arrogant).   He is always accessible and welcomes questions and discussions. A co-worker and I have called him "sensei" and "Yoda", which fits, but perhaps doesn't quite express the level of respect that I believe he deserves. I endeavor to have others think of me the way I think of my mentor. Knowledge and education are not equal to wisdom. While they certainly may contribute, I see wisdom as a complete package of knowledge, experience, accessibility, and an ability to communicate a message to anyone using words and expressions that will make the message clear to the recipient. It's all about the other person, not self. You can't guide Marines (or anyone, for that matter) to success with Lean Six Sigma without wisdom. It takes that special mixture to enter a command with a mission you've never supported, people you've never met, and help them see the vision of what they could achieve with Lean Six Sigma – to teach them, guide them around road blocks, recognize patterns for quick reaction, and know when to coach and when to let go.

It seems the right mixture of characteristics: respectfully joining those who have mastered Honor, Courage, and Commitment with Lean Six Sigma experts who have optimism, humility, and wisdom.

First Things First – Top Cover

Once our small group of enthusiastic process improvers at Marine Corps Headquarters decided this was absolutely the right thing for our beloved Corps, there were some obvious and necessary steps to take. Even the best ideas and intentions do not go far in a large organization (particularly a large military organization) without buy-in from the top. Fortunately, leaders at the Department of Defense in appointed positions had come from private industry. They were familiar and comfortable with Lean Six Sigma. In fact, the Honorable Gordon England[15], Deputy Secretary of Defense, had already initiated Lean Six Sigma for the Department of Defense. His directive was then followed by supporting memorandums from the Department of the Navy (DON). A couple of us participated on the DON process improvement

---

[15] The Honorable Gordon England served as the 29th Deputy Secretary of Defense, under President George W. Bush, from January 2006 to February 2009. An engineer by education, Mr. England held several leadership positions across various sectors of the General Dynamics Corporation.

leadership team, known as the Transformation Team Leader (TTL) forum, whose mission was to "coordinate [process improvement] strategy and tactics among the major stakeholders". True to form, proudly accomplishing more with less, I was often the only Marine Corps representative at the table: a mid-level civilian amongst Admirals and Senior Executives.

Once DoD and DON produced Lean Six Sigma guidance (aka Continuous Process Improvement, or CPI) in May of 2006, it was not difficult to gain support from our sitting Assistant Commandant of the Marine Corps by way of a message, introducing our formal approach to process improvement across the Corps. The title of this December 2006 message: "Improving Combat Readiness through Innovation". What a great Christmas gift. Our Lean Six Sigma work had officially begun.

Lighting the Fire

Is there an organization in existence with more young people per capita who have more energy and vigor than the Marine Corps? If so, I don't know of it. Given this scenario as a starting point, consider the response when a single Marine or small group of Marines finds a new idea (toolset) that provides quick results and gains the attention of the boss, in a good way, and makes the participant feel as if he or she has made a quick, measurable, sustainable, and concrete difference. It's not just like a spark to a forest; it's more like a spark to a gasoline doused drought-ridden forest.

We considered multiple times developing a marketing strategy for the Lean Six Sigma program. Each attempt made limited progress, due to such a small team with such a great demand. Marketing was lower in priority than training and mentoring Marines. We just didn't have the time!

In all actuality, there is no better marketing plan than success. At one installation, Marines in an outdoor maintenance bay improved their local processes and re-designed the layout of their maintenance area and tool storage. What do you think the Marines in the next bay opted to do? Ignore the visible improvements next door? Absolutely not.

This is a very supportive yet competitive environment. Success spreads like wildfire.

Often, the improvements are not new ideas. They are thoughts and ideas that have existed for weeks, months, or even years. As I repeatedly find myself saying, "this is not rocket science". The simplest solutions are often the best.

Layers in the chain-of-command, which need to exist due to what is asked of Marines and leadership, often prevent good ideas initiated on the ground floor from being heard by the top brass. Younger Marines, who are truly the subject matter experts when it comes to day-to-day actions, can easily describe "areas of pain". Rather than use consultant-ease, I like to approach people and ask them about their regular headaches, what they do on a regular or semi-regular basis that they don't like, or even dread? Humans have a natural aversion to inefficiency and waste. When we feel like we are wasting time or energy, we don't like it. The risk, especially in a military environment where orders are followed with little questioning, is that people will do as directed, even if the process is bad, and just end up with a sense of not liking the process. Inevitably when asked why they participate over and over in a process that is bad, the answer is along the lines of "we have always done it that way", or "I was told to…".

When Lean Six Sigma quickly cures the headache or headaches of Marines, they tell others about it, and the fire spreads. When the boss gets wind of the good process results achieved by Marines, and mentions this to other Marines, the fire spreads. When Marines hold a friendly competition for best results, the fire spreads. It's an exhilarating environment.

PART 3. A BIT OF HOW-TO: HOW IT'S DONE

– "Because of this…, I think that I am a better leader."
LSS Green Belt Student, December 2010, Marine Corps Air
Station Miramar

When reading this section of the book, please consider your organization or situation. It matters not how large or small, the mission or industry. The description below can be scaled to ANY organization. You can use this approach in ANY setting. I have literally used Lean Six Sigma with my recurring processes ("headaches") at home – and yes, this includes laundry and the messy garage. During these years with the Marine Corps, I have been involved with Lean Six Sigma at the unit level, battalion level, regiment level, major command level, and Headquarters level. I have personally trained senior leaders, middle management, young enlisted Marines, and even high school students. I have worked with plumbers, electricians, Generals, administrative assistants, warehouse experts, inspectors, medical personnel, commanding officers, supply clerks, and the list goes on.

This approach and these tools work anywhere and with anyone. This approach I am sharing with you is a <u>simple</u> model. But, I won't ever say it is <u>easy</u>.

Getting Started

When starting something new that is <u>so exciting</u>, there is a significant risk of making the deadly mistake of progressing in the wrong order: READY – FIRE! – AIM.

We tried very hard to follow a disciplined approach to ensure that the program didn't get ahead of its maturity, or our capability. This involved a thoughtful gathering of resources and a roll-out plan. While a few contractors and consultants were already available, our goal was to develop organic capability to link LSS skill with Marine Corps experience and knowledge, further ensuring long term success. We sought out experts, including a contract with experienced LSS Master Black Belts who could train and mentor our internal team members through our program's first few years.

In the austere Marine Corps environment, supporting nearly 200,000 Marines and 33,000 civilians, we hired a Lean Six Sigma contractor who brought us five LSS Master Black Belts. Their purpose was not to fish for us, but rather, to teach us to fish. This is an invaluable model.

I recommend that if you plan to initiate a Lean Six Sigma program in your organization, hire an expert or two for the first period, to train people, guide leaders, and help get things moving along the right path. True experts have seen successes and failures, can protect you from common mistakes, and can ultimately save time and money for your organization. But watch out, there are plenty of charlatans: as in any business there are people who pose as experts, and may even have the right academic knowledge, but without real experience.

In addition to bringing a few experts on-board, our program established foundational documentation:

- Written Order – The purpose of the written order is to disseminate the overall plan to the organization, and to let everyone know that this is coming from the top. This might be in the form of a company memo or message from the President or Owner. I completely enjoyed reading about Jack Welch's approach with GE in 1997, when he basically told his leadership that they were welcome to choose whether or not to embrace the new Six Sigma program. But, if they chose not to embrace it, they would be doing so from somewhere else[16]. In other words: join us, or leave. That's a pretty clear message.

- Guidebook – This is the "how-to" manual for your organization. It describes the nuts and bolts of how the program will run. It includes an introduction, key terms defined, timeline, training descriptions, examples, resources, certification requirements, and so on.

---

[16] See Slater, chapter 12. Slater, Robert. *The GE Way Fieldbook*. New York: McGraw-Hill, 2000. Print.

Lean to the Corps

- Templates – A well thought-out program includes foundational templates for practitioners. Templates can be standard formats for briefs, tables, project documentation, agreements, reporting, etc. These most likely will change and improve over time, based on local needs, experience, and maturity. If templates for commonly used tools, communication, reporting, etc. are not established from the beginning, the inventive players will develop their own, which sounds like a great idea, until the end of the year when you would like to combine individual results to show program success and find that you can't; or would like to report top projects to leaders or shareholders and find that the briefs, metrics, and presentations vary so much that the format is unfamiliar and distracts from content; or less experienced team members get overwhelmed with lack of guidance and simply give up. Templates not only provide a professional appearance for information, but they are also excellent guides for the players, defining what information is needed, or containing examples for clarity.
- Training – Basic types of training must be identified, sources of content and delivery settled, and a timeline set. Once a plan to engage in Lean Six Sigma is developed, the first action with employees is typically training. The following are the types of training we established as our standard set:
  - "Deskside" Brief – A one-on-one introduction for senior leaders, typically held in his or her office, often with key personnel present, explaining the concepts of Lean Six Sigma and concluding with a decision of go/no go for the local organization.
  - Senior Leader Training – An introduction to Lean Six Sigma which is scheduled by the top leader, following the Deskside meeting, for all of the senior leaders and possibly middle management. Length of training is typically 4-8 hours, covering purpose of Lean Six Sigma within the organization, history of LSS, roles and responsibilities for

deploying LSS, introduction to Lean, introduction to Six Sigma, and possibly an exercise or two.

o LSS White Belt Training – A one to two-hour basic introduction to Lean Six Sigma principles which is useful for anyone in general, potential LSS Green and Black Belts, and Leadership or Stakeholders. In our case, this particular training had already been established by the Navy as an on-line class, which we were able to access. Perfect!

o LSS Yellow Belt Training – An eight to sixteen-hour introduction to Lean Six Sigma principles (with exercises) which is useful for Project Team members, potential LSS Green and Black Belts, and Leadership or Stakeholders. We opted to provide this training in a traditional classroom setting, with fun exercises (involving Legos!). The class was developed to be informative, fun, and interest generating for those who have a natural inclination toward Lean Six Sigma.

o LSS Green Belt Training – A forty-hour class on basic Lean and Six Sigma tools, addressing the standard body of knowledge published by American Society for Quality, the gold standard for Lean Six Sigma. This is the first level of training officially recognized in industry (LSS White and Yellow Belt level courses are simply introductory and can contain any sort of curriculum, although as of late, Yellow Belt has received attention and may be more regulated in the future.) The LSS Green Belt credential has a specific meaning, which is recognized and understood world-wide. This is the first official level of training and certification for Lean Six Sigma practitioners, and includes a comprehensive exam at the conclusion of class. The class is designed to prepare students to facilitate process improvement teams, lead smaller scoped projects, and hold key roles in larger scoped projects that are led by LSS Black Belts and Master Black Belts. Once practical experience is obtained, the LSS Green Belt may train team members and possibly coach or mentor other LSS Green Belts. Many smaller organizations who do not have LSS Black Belts on staff are able to accomplish quite a lot by training employees who are local process experts to also serve as LSS Green Belts. As Lean Six Sigma has grown and become more popular, the supply of training resources has increased. LSS Green Belt classes are provided by colleges, universities, consultant firms, and professional organizations. The good news is that the cost of training has decreased, and there are many good resources available. The bad news is that some of the training providers do not offer a high-quality product. An organization seeking training should find a reputable resource, with actual project experience in addition to academic knowledge, and verifiable references. An aspect of the training we provided, and I believe a key factor for our success, is the "mentoring" support model. All graduating LSS Green Belt students are assigned an experienced LSS Black Belt or Master Black Belt to provide guidance and support during first project work following class. The mentors provide planning support, templates, training, etc., to help the inexperienced LSS Green Belts gain experience and avoid common pitfalls. LSS Green Belts serve as the organization's Lean Six Sigma "backbone", due to sheer numbers. There are often 10 LSS Green Belts for every LSS Black Belt in an organization. In the Marine Corps, the ratio is much more extreme.

o LSS Black Belt Training – This 160-hour course also covers a standard body of knowledge, published by American Society for Quality. This is the second official level of training and certification for Lean Six Sigma practitioners, and includes a comprehensive exam at the conclusion of class. While training providers and organizations roll-out the training in a variety of ways, we opted to deliver each LSS Black Belt course series with a forty-hour class one week per month over a period of four months[17]. Students are expected to be experienced LSS Green Belts in order to attend the LSS Black Belt class. Due to the heavy emphasis on statistics, students are provided with a pre-test addressing the basic math skills necessary to successfully complete the LSS Black Belt training. While the majority of training content is focused on LSS tools, and process or data analysis, a few additional skill areas are also addressed: project management, facilitation, and inter-personal skills. Students arrive to class with a work process that has been identified to improve, and will facilitate a process improvement team during the four-month class period, serving as their first LSS Black Belt project. The model involves one week of training, followed by three weeks at student's work location performing normal duties and facilitating a project using tools and techniques taught in class, followed by another week of class, etc. At the conclusion of the final week of class, students report results or planned results for their projects. As with LSS Green Belt training, all LSS Black Belts are assigned an experienced LSS Black Belt or Master Black Belt to serve as a mentor. LSS Black Belts are expected to lead larger scoped projects, train LSS Green Belts, coach and mentor less experienced practitioners, and often are full-time Lean Six Sigma experts for an organization. LSS Black Belts may seek certification, which is a credential of proven expertise, similar to Professional Engineering license for engineers or

---

[17] It should be noted that in 2012, due to a significant budget cut known as "sequestration", the Marine Corps placed all LSS Black Belt training courses on hold until an undecided future date. All LSS Black Belt training beyond that point has been provided by external sources.

Certified Public Accountant title for accountants. The best option for this credential is application and testing through the American Society for Quality[18].

o LSS Mentor Workshop – I have personally developed and provided mentoring training for new and perspective mentors (as described above, assigned to support new LSS Green Belts and Black Belts), which can be taught in a one to two-hour session. This involves a review of key curriculum elements to ensure that mentors have a clear understanding of what is currently being taught in LSS Green Belt and Black Belt class, as well as recommended levels of support based on experience and needs of the "mentee". In 2012, the Marine Corps' Lean Six Sigma program developed a standard mentor training package with an emphasis on coaching and mentoring techniques rather than content of LSS training. Both mentoring training approaches are fine options.

o Other Training – While many enthusiastic practitioners have sought out supplemental training and additional process improvement tools, the list above is conclusive. As mentioned in the first chapter of this book, there is a risk associated with seeking out good tools to the detriment of great tools. The idea is to keep Lean Six Sigma as THE approach for process improvement, and continue to get better at implementing it. Be careful about introducing conflicting or competitive tools through training.

- Schedule – As any good project manager worth his salt will tell you, all projects and plans need to start with a high level "Plan of Action and Milestones", or POAM. We developed a notional POAM, that has adjusted and changed over time, as they all do. Key milestones included in the plan were: accessing expertise through

---

[18] See details at www.asq.org

contract, developing internal resources for LSS Black Belt and Master Black Belt capability, discontinuing contract support, engaging with Headquarters leadership and all Marine Corps installations, to name a few. As with any work breakdown structure, we then developed the steps necessary to reach those milestones. A plan was born. The plan included time periods, which ultimately served as a schedule.

- Assignments – Determining responsibilities at the outset wasn't a difficult task, because we just didn't have enough people to make it difficult. We worked side-by-side to get everything done. We naturally progressed to a regional model for support: team members in the National Capitol Region to support Headquarters and higher commands, a team in North Carolina supporting the rest of the east coast, San Diego supporting the southwest region, a team member in Hawaii and another in Japan. It was a logical distribution of talent and support. We remained a relatively flat organization, owned by Headquarters, with significant partnering across installation business offices. By 2006, our LSS contract was in place, staff had been hired, and roles and responsibilities were being molded and developed. Then our director departed to support work in Afghanistan, and a new director was named, along with an assistant and head Master Black Belt for the Marine Corps. The program continued to evolve and mature.

- Web-based Management – In order to make process improvement visible across the entire Marine Corps, a management information system was adopted. The particular software that was selected had already been established for the private sector. The Army and Air Force had adopted and tailored the tool. The Navy then joined in with the Marine Corps closely behind. In the early days, we shared ideas and desires for the web tool. People much more competent than I helped to tailor the tool for broad use. The result was an established Navy/Marine Corps stand-alone web-based clearinghouse for Lean Six Sigma tools and tracking. I often find myself wondering if we would have been better off to use the off-the-shelf version of the tool rather than adjusting it with too many specifications. We may never know, but it has been a fantastic tool for visibility, communication, and tracking of personnel. Project tools and templates can be found on our LSS website. A key word search reveals projects and files that have been loaded and are associated with the key words (such as "warehouse" or "radio maintenance" or "Joe Smith"). The tool is used by certifiers to review project documentation of those who are seeking certification. Training files and practitioner templates are loaded and available. Once a practitioner has been trained at the LSS Green Belt level, username and password are established for easy access to this warehouse of information.

Infrastructure

I am a fan of Deming[19]. I studied process improvement in college in the 1980's, with Deming as the godfather of process improvement (along with Ishikawa and Shingo). I surfed the Total Quality Management[20] wave, and loved the possibilities associated with broad process improvement. But once I left academia and entered the real world of work, I found that process improvement was often disjointed or after achieving some success, seemed to fizzle. The tools and concepts were solid, so why were the results not perpetual?

It's a hard nut to crack. The easy answer is that people are "resistant to change". If I had a nickel for every time I have heard this phrase, or even used it myself, well, I'd have a ton of nickels. But, honestly, people are really more resistant to looking silly or being ridiculed than to actual change. They don't want to feel like the lone

---

[19] W. Edwards Deming, renowned engineer and physicist who influenced process improvement in the United States as well as Japan prior to his death in 1993.

[20] Total Quality Management (TQM) was a predecessor to Lean Six Sigma. Many of the tools are the same, but the standard approach or methodology (such as DMAIC) was missing.

guy or gal on the battlefield. Stepping out is much easier, and more comfortable, with support. People need mentors!

We purposely developed an infrastructure where EVERY SINGLE PERSON who engaged with Lean Six Sigma had a more experienced person to lean on or contact when a question arose, or when trying out a new tool or template. I can name my person, and I expect that nearly 100% of people I have trained at the LSS Green Belt or Black Belt level, or leaders we have engaged for Lean Six Sigma involvement, can provide the name of their "expert". That's the true infrastructure. Sure, there are Directors and Leads for this and that. Most programs have a similar set up. But, I challenge you to find a movement such as Lean Six Sigma that has lasted beyond introduction and initial excitement (or enforcement) without an intentionally designed infrastructure of support. I believe this is why TQM didn't last, and Lean Six Sigma has become perpetual in some organizations. There are countless variables, and snipers that can kill a good Lean Six Sigma program. But, if Lean Six Sigma is to last, the most important element is a mentoring and support infrastructure.

In addition, there are always politics and personal opinions that affect the directions of organizations. A simple, yet solid infrastructure model can help your Lean Six Sigma program withstand changes in leadership, strategy, or even financial outlook. You see, once process improvement becomes engrained in your organization's culture, and people grow to be familiar with the simple approach to process improvement, and mentors abound, it becomes a natural part of your everyday working environment. Change in market? Lean Six Sigma still applies. Change in managing board of directors? Lean Six Sigma is still the best tool to reduce waste and standardize processes. Change in cash flow? Lean Six Sigma is the best way to reduce costs to respond to resource shortages or deal with new demand. It applies to ANY process in ANY organization.

In addition to the simple mentoring model we have discussed, I would recommend training your staff and generally approaching opportunities for improvement as follows (or some hybrid of this basic approach):

1) Train every single person in the organization at the introductory level (we use the terms LSS White Belt and Yellow Belt level training)

2) For those who really enjoy the training, and feel as though they are a natural fit with Lean Six Sigma, allow them to volunteer for the next level of training: LSS Green Belt

3) For those LSS Green Belts who produce results and enjoy running Lean Six Sigma projects, allow them to volunteer for the next level of training: LSS Black Belt

4) When at all possible, allow LSS Black Belts to work as Lean Six Sigma experts on a full-time basis (permanently, or possibly for a multi-year assignment).

5) Follow project results in visible ways (wall graphics in key locations, newsletters, standard meeting agenda item for leadership, etc.) so that everyone knows this is of value to leadership.

6) For anything that causes your organization pain or headaches – ANYTHING – ask "what process(es) is involved with this pain or headache?" and "can we improve this process with Lean Six Sigma?" HINT: The answer is always YES!

7) Also, as a bonus gift to you, the reader, I will share a secret: those who are really good at Lean Six Sigma, and produce results, are the people you want to promote in your organization. You can't have success as a LSS practitioner on a continuing basis without being quick on your feet, a natural leader, and someone who others choose to follow. Unpleasant and negative people do not typically experience success as LSS facilitators on an on-going basis. Insincere or unscrupulous people also can't seem to keep up the façade. Only the genuine leaders experience continued success*. So, if you make LSS Black Belt or even Green Belt capability criteria (whether you announce it or keep it secret) for advancement in your organization, you will benefit.

*Note: I am not suggesting that a single project that fails or doesn't reach completion is equal to failure. Many projects do not reach completion due to factors out of the facilitator's control. What I am suggesting is that a successful practitioner continues to look for the next opportunity for improvement and has others who are more than willing to follow along, naturally.

When a project fails, you are looking for the Babe Ruth attitude: "Every strike brings me closer to the next home run."

8) This approach is not necessarily EASY, but it is definitely SIMPLE!

Training and Mentoring

Have you ever known someone with "book smarts", but not "street smarts" on a topic? You know, they've studied or read about it, but have never actually <u>done</u> it. If you were planning to engage in activity related to that topic, would you seek advice from the book smart person, or would you prefer someone with street smarts? Personally, I prefer advice from someone with both!

This is the training and mentoring model: everyone is supported by someone who has more knowledge and experience. We discussed mentoring earlier, but this is important, so let's dig a little deeper. As alluded to earlier, establishing an infrastructure of support is critical to long-term success (honestly, for any program, not just Lean Six Sigma).

As you pursue Lean Six Sigma, every person in your organization should be able to identify someone else BY NAME who is their go-to person for LSS help. This "mentor" should be at least one level of training and experience beyond the one seeking support.

The best way to manage and assign the training and mentoring personnel is during actual training:

1) Mentor Pool: Keep a current list of people who have been trained at each level (Lean Six Sigma White Belt, Yellow Belt, Green Belt, and Black Belt). Also keep track of certification[21] levels, if applicable.

2) Introductory Support: For personnel who have participated in introductory level training ("Deskside", Senior Leader, LSS White Belt, or LSS Yellow Belt), the

---

[21] Many organizations opt to pursue certifications in addition to training at the LSS Green Belt, Black Belt, and Master Black Belt levels. Certifications are earned when the practitioner not only completes training and typically a comprehensive exam, but also a set number of successful projects. Thus, certification addresses training, knowledge, and experience.

training instructor provides contact information, and is available for questions and further support.

3) LSS Green Belt Mentors:
   a. For personnel who attend LSS Green Belt training, a mentor is identified prior to the conclusion of training.
   b. The class roster, provided to all students, contains a mentor name for each student, along with contact information.
   c. Students then engage with mentor following completion of class, for support during first few projects.
   d. Mentors for LSS Green Belts are either LSS Black Belts or Master Black Belts with project experience or possibly very experienced LSS Green Belts.

4) LSS Black Belt Mentors:
   a. A mentor is identified for each student prior to initiation of LSS Black Belt training.
   b. The mentor contacts the student prior to class to help prepare, including developing a draft project charter. Students are expected to complete a project from their local work area (see LSS Black Belt training description discussed earlier) during the period of LSS Black Belt training. The project charter is the description of that project (and, of course, there is a standard charter template!).
   c. The mentor may also provide a math quiz/review to identify and address any skill gaps prior to training.
   d. During the training period, the mentor provides project support and ensures the student uses recommended Lean Six Sigma tools and completes any required documentation.
   e. After training, the mentor continues to provide support, when requested.
   f. Mentors for LSS Black Belts are LSS Master Black Belts or possibly very experienced LSS Black Belts.

5) LSS Master Black Belt Mentors: "Every person" means EVERYONE. Even LSS Master Black Belts benefit from having an assigned mentor, or perhaps colleague. Experts

join together for all sorts of reasons and benefits (ever heard of a "Think Tank"?). By the time a Lean Six Sigma practitioner reaches LSS Master Black Belt level, he or she will have many available resources for support. But, as a standard practice for your organization, even LSS Master Black Belts should have an identified mentor.

6) Mentor Guidance:
   a. All mentors should receive formal or informal mentor training prior to acting in this capacity, in order to understand expectations.
   b. Definitions of mentoring support should be developed, such as:
      i. Maximum Support: When needed, attend team meetings, help facilitate, provide coaching prior to and after team meetings. This is typically for the new LSS Green Belt with zero experience.
      ii. Moderate Support: Regularly visit or call "mentee" to check on status and offer support. Mentor engages regularly with mentee.
      iii. Minimum Support: Remain on call when "mentee" has questions or reaches roadblocks. Mentor waits until called upon by mentee. This is typically for the experienced LSS Green Belt or Black Belt.
   c. A feedback mechanism should be established to allow "mentees" to evaluate the support provided by the mentor.

This is a rather simple model. It may be best to designate a person to track and manage mentor/mentee assignments. Visibility is always a good thing: if possible, post mentor/mentee pools, lists, and rosters in a standard location allowing easy access by everyone.

Remember, this infrastructure of support may be what makes or breaks your Lean Six Sigma program. If managed and adhered to faithfully, your probability of success increases greatly. Think of this as the skeleton of the LSS program. Without it, you just have an unstable, wobbly mass. Who wants that?

Top-Down vs. Bottom-Up

We've discussed training and mentoring, to prepare people and support Lean Six Sigma work. But, how do you decide <u>what</u> work to do, and beyond that... <u>what should be first</u>??

TOP-DOWN PROJECT IDENTIFICATION

In a perfect world, the boss in charge discovers this wonderful approach called Lean Six Sigma, calls in a few experts along with local leaders to develop a plan, brings everyone else in the organization in on the plan, and proceeds to establish and run a Lean Six Sigma program – resulting in great success and world supremacy in their particular skill or market niche.

Perhaps a bit of an exaggeration, but in this scenario, the top person or persons in the organization embraced the concept of Lean Six Sigma and led the organization from the top. Thus, "Top-Down".

A more realistic scenario, and one I have seen in the Marine Corps multiple times within commands, goes a bit like this:

- The Commanding Officer (CO) has seen or heard of Lean Six Sigma via personal training, a deskside brief, or a subordinate who brings it to his or her attention.
- LSS experts from our HQ office then meet with the CO and local leadership to develop a list of first projects. The working meeting follows this approach:
  - Review mission of the organization
  - Identify "customers" of the organization (who benefits or receives outputs from the organization?)
  - Discuss customer requirements
  - Review any current measurements of performance
  - Identify any gaps in performance (Are there any areas where customers are not receiving what they require? Any areas where mission is difficult to accomplish?)
  - Identify any other recurring "headaches" within the organization (What are some recurring requirements that are just painful to do? – These are probably associated with broken, or inefficient,

processes. People do not like to work with a bad process, and often do not even realize that the problem is a bad process.)

- o Discuss processes associated with the performance gaps and headaches
- o Prioritize these processes, worst first (I purposely don't define "worst". To some people this may mean most costly, to others it may mean most difficult, the interpretations are endless. But, the point is to get some sort of agreement as to which are the greatest problems for the organization.)
- o Now we have a list of potential projects (based on identified processes).
- o Rough project planning comes next (this is done for each of the top potential projects):
  - Who is in charge of the process?
  - Who works within the process?
  - Are there any current measurements associated with the process?
  - If so, what are the current values?
  - Establish a simple statement of the process issue(s).
  - Establish a simple goal (or goals) for improvement.
  - Determine the best timing to get started with this particular project.

- The meeting described above results in a list of first projects, and enough content to begin training and preparing teams to meet and work on their assigned processes. I have used the "Flip Chart Guide" on the following pages to help facilitators prepare for project identification meetings. The rectangles represent individual pages of chart paper placed on the meeting room wall in order to visibly document the working session discussion. Note that while all pages are developed prior to the meeting, content on the working session charts, with red and blue titles, is developed during the meeting. This is typically a two to four hour working session.

Lean to the Corps

Project Identification Workshop Flip Chart Guide:

Support Chart: Purpose

PURPOSE

- Document Key Processes, Customers and Current Performance
- Identify Issues, Performance Gaps, and "Areas of Pain"
- Develop list of potential projects to address Issues, Performance Gaps, and "Areas of Pain"

Support Chart: Agenda

AGENDA

- ☐ INTRODUCTIONS
- ☐ PURPOSE
- ☐ CPI BACKGROUND/ ORG BACKGROUND
- ☐ WORKING SESSION
  - o Mission
  - o Core Value Streams
  - o Products and Services
  - o Customers
  - o Customer Requirements
  - o Current Performance
  - o Gaps and Other "Areas of Pain"
  - o Project Ideas
  - o Project Details
- ☐ NEXT STEPS

Support Chart: Next Steps

NEXT STEPS

- Meeting Documentation
- Group Review
- Revisions
- Inform Other Stakeholders
- Develop Project Charters
- Coordinate Project Teams
- Agree on Start Date/ Timeline
- Train, As Needed
- Begin Projects

Working Session Chart 1: Mission

MISSION

Working Session Chart 2: Core Value Streams

CORE VALUE STREAMS
(Key Processes)

Working Session Chart 3: Products & Services

PRODUCTS & SERVICES

Working Session Chart 4: Customers

CUSTOMERS

Working Session Chart 5: Customer Requirements

CUSTOMER REQUIREMENTS

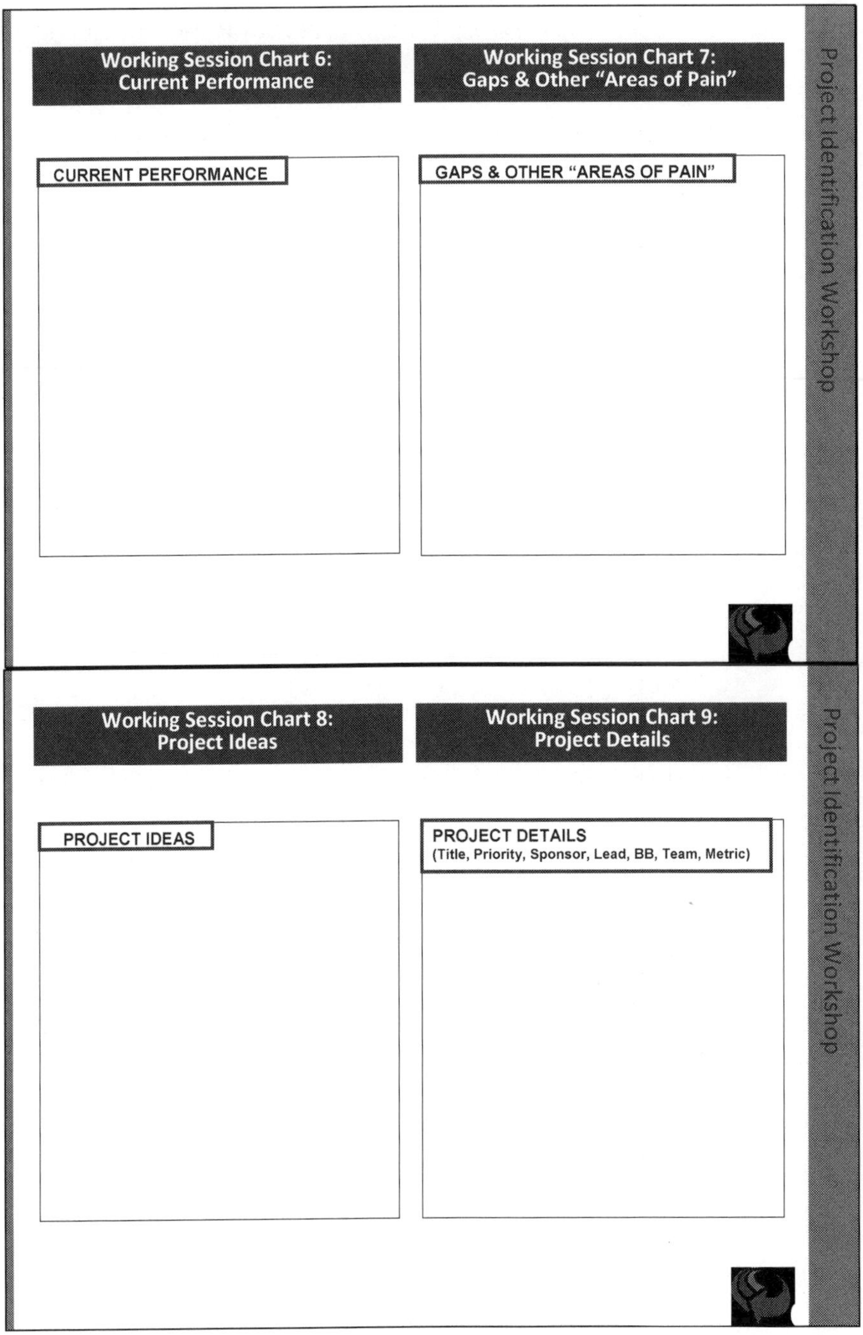
Working Session Chart 6:
Current Performance
Working Session Chart 7:
Gaps & Other "Areas of Pain"
CURRENT PERFORMANCE
GAPS & OTHER "AREAS OF PAIN"
Project Identification Workshop
Working Session Chart 8:
Project Ideas
Working Session Chart 9:
Project Details
PROJECT IDEAS
PROJECT DETAILS
(Title, Priority, Sponsor, Lead, BB, Team, Metric)
Project Identification Workshop

Figure 3 Project Identification Workshop Flip Chart Guide

- Training ensues:
  - LSS White Belt (on-line) training information is disseminated to all.
  - LSS Yellow Belt training is provided for all personnel who will be working on first projects.
  - LSS Green Belt training is provided to personnel who have been selected to facilitate the project teams.
  - And in best cases, an additional training session will be provided for those in the organization who are in charge of the processes being addressed. Further information is provided in the "Running a Project" section, below.
- Teams are established to address each project.
- First projects are initiated either all together, or staggered, based on capacity and leadership choice.
- Status and final results are reported to leadership on a regular basis (a regularly scheduled standing meeting is best).
- As projects conclude and results are managed longer term, additional projects are kicked off.
- Project list is reviewed and updated on a regular basis, using the approach described above.
- This can and should be a continuous loop for formal process improvement.
- The entire approach is scalable: it works for large organizations, subsets of organizations, small businesses, families, you name it!

BOTTOM-UP PROJECT IDENTIFICATION:

Top down is always best, but sometimes the top brass needs a little help recognizing a good thing so proof of concept is also a respectable approach. I have seen this approach work many times, as well.

- Boss or Marine is told by a friend about, or expresses interest in Lean Six Sigma.

- With permission, he or she attends training at the LSS Green Belt level (and often has attended LSS Yellow Belt training prior).
- LSS trained Green Belt then selects a local process to improve and completes a project.
- Results are reported up the chain-of-command.
- Interest is generated, once concept of Lean Six Sigma is proven locally. (Concrete results are a must – don't be the used car salesman, with false or questionable data. If you need help identifying a good way to show results, check with your mentor, of course!)
- At this point, either more people seek out training and individual projects, or leadership takes over and the "Top-Down" approach ensues.

Often with the "Bottom-Up" approach, process improvement becomes a friendly competition of sorts. One group improves their local process(es) or the appearance of their work area, then the group next door wants to do the same, then the next group... process improvement is contagious. Trust me, this is a really fun environment for work. People are proud of their accomplishments, work becomes more enjoyable, and work relationships strengthen with a true sense of team and pride. It's all good!

Running a Project

We've discussed Lean Six Sigma at the program level, and managing groups of projects, but what is the recipe to actually run a single project? I will share my approach for simple (or smaller-scoped) projects. And, in my experience, most projects are simple (see examples in the next section of this book). Even in highly efficient companies, such as Toyota or Motorola, there are mostly simple processes to address, if scoped as such. More complex processes can often be divided up into manageable "chunks", as long as solutions are put in place with the entire process in mind. This concept will become easier to understand and manage with a bit of experience. In the meantime, call on your mentor!

Please note, some of the nuances described here are based on my opinions, which are backed up by education, experience, and a portfolio of over 100 Lean Six Sigma projects and events. Many people in the Marine Corps have adopted this approach, so I believe it has proven to be effective. Some of the steps/tools mentioned below may not be familiar to readers who have not attended Lean Six Sigma training. A quick internet search, or review of recommended reading at the end of this book may be of assistance.

Warning: Even with this recipe, I recommend that you always call on more experienced help when starting out. This may mean hiring a contractor or consultant, or seeking an experienced Lean Six Sigma expert in your organization. Expert guidance significantly increases your probability of success, particularly at first! Also, do not attempt to lead or facilitate a LSS project without the proper training. In our organization, team facilitators are trained at least as Green Belts (forty hours of training).

Recipe for a Project:
1) Identify project topic (from Top Down vs. Bottom Up discussion earlier in this chapter).
2) Select and train team (also discussed earlier).
3) Review documented projects, if they exist, to see what others have done to improve similar processes.
4) Develop Project Charter (a standard template for all of your organization's charters is best, to allow for ease of understanding, communication, and consolidation). The Charter is the guiding document for the team, and is

considered a "living document", which means that it may need to be adjusted as the process is studied and better understood. A good charter should be kept to one or two pages, and contains:

    a. Title of process

    b. Organization or section of organization affected

    c. Date of charter

    d. Numbering or naming convention, if one has been developed to manage LSS projects

    e. Process owner (who has the authority to make the changes recommended by team)

    f. Project facilitator (LSS Green Belt or Black Belt, and sometimes Master Black Belt)

    g. Problem or opportunity statement – This should be only a statement of the problem, and no potential solutions. It should be one to two paragraphs with quantitative descriptions where possible. This means instead of saying "The process takes too long.", further detail is provided, such as "The ABC process currently takes X hours to complete, which results in Y% of deliveries being late. This has occurred for Z months…"

    h. Goal of the project – My simple model is "Improve <metric> from <current value> to <target value> by <date>." Where the metric is your primary concern described in the problem statement (most likely associated with cost, time, or quality).

    i. Team members – By name and role.

    j. Timing of project – When to begin, conclude, and any other key milestones.

    k. Scope of project – For example "This project addresses the ABC process beginning with <first step> and ending with <ending step>." Also include specifics on "Out of Scope" elements, if applicable: "This project will not address…".

    l. As a bonus, a signature line for the process owner or higher management is often helpful, to show team members and others that this is important to leadership.

Project Charter		Date Initiated:
Organization		Revision Date:
Project Title		

1. Project Information

Senior Leader:	Project ☐	Just Do It ☐
Project Sponsor:	RIE ☐	Other ☐
Project Facilitator (Green/Black Belt):		
Estimated Start Date:	Project ID #:	
Estimated End Date:	Parent Project ID #:	

2. Problem Statement

3. Goal Statement

4. Project Scope

In Scope ...	Out of Scope ...

5. Team Members

Name	Role	Organization

6. Approvals/Signatures

	Signature	Date
Black Belt/Green Belt		
BB/MBB Mentor		
Project Sponsor		
Senior Leader		

Figure 4 Sample Charter Format

5) Once the Project Charter is drafted, typically by the LSS facilitator and process owner, review with the team during first team meeting. Drafting the charter ahead saves team time and gains process owner buy-in. Reviewing and

allowing team involvement gains subject matter expert scrutiny and establishes team ownership of the charter.

6) Conduct the following steps during team meetings, using the Define-Measure-Analyze-Improve-Control (DMAIC) model. I have developed this STREAMLINED LEAN SIX SIGMA approach over several years. While it can be tailored, I believe the following represents the cleanest and fastest way to complete a LSS project.

    a. DEFINE:
        i. Kick-off project – Have process owner or manager stop in for first five to ten minutes to describe why team members were selected and why this is important to the organization.
        ii. Introduce team, if applicable.
        iii. Introduce team meeting approach – I prefer to use flip chart paper and butcher paper on the walls, write with thick marker, and ensure that all team members can see what is being discussed in order to stay engaged. *Author's Note: This is not a book on facilitation, but the facilitator should always be standing. By sitting at the end of a table and writing or typing using media that can't be seen by participants, you are giving them permission to check out of the conversation and you are also increasing your chances of failure!*
        iv. Start a running list of "Issues" – These are current problems with the process. Team members will arrive ready, willing, and anxious to discuss what is wrong with the process. These discussions are a rich source of information. As the facilitator, allow some discussion, document the issues (on the wall), then return team to agenda. As meetings continue, more issues will be

mentioned. Simply keep adding to the issues list and return team to agenda.

v. Start a running list of "Ideas" – In addition to problems, team members will most likely arrive with solutions. It's in our human nature to fix problems. But, with Lean Six Sigma, we don't jump to conclusions. We must first follow a disciplined approach to understand the process, which may send the team in an unexpected direction for final solutions. This is always interesting and fun! So, when an idea is mentioned, add it to the ideas list and get back on topic.

vi. Create a summary of the process – This allows all team members to clearly understand what is being addressed. A good tool for this is called SIPOC, which identifies Suppliers, Inputs, high level Process steps, Outputs, and Customers of the process. Sample SIPOC pictures are provided in the following chapter.

vii. Conduct an "Issues exercise" – Taking the existing issues list, direct team to brainstorm and identify additional problems or issues with the current process. Once a solid list is created, have team vote on top issues. The result is a prioritized list of issues. The team should then strive to address the top issues by the conclusion of the project.

b. MEASURE:

i. Map the current process – The product of this step is often called a process map, or flow chart, or value stream map. This is possibly the MOST IMPORTANT step of a process improvement project. This exercise is an eye-opening experience and nearly always results in one or two team members exclaiming "I didn't know you do that!" or

"Why do we do it that way?". The "process map", which is the next generation of our old friend the "flow chart", should be at a level of detail that clearly shows the steps that individuals take in the process. In addition to steps, it is helpful to document who conducts each step, timing associated with the steps, and tools/templates/guidance used for each step. There is both an art and a science to developing good process maps. It's helpful to have an experienced LSS facilitator assist.

  ii. Walk the process – In addition to discussing and mapping the process in a meeting room, take the team on a little field trip. Go and visit the workers in the process. Travel in the order of the process, if possible. Gather a bit of "intel" during this exercise: ask the workers what issues they see with the current process and if they have any recommendations. Where should this information ultimately be documented? You got it – the Issues and Ideas lists.

  iii. Develop a data collection plan and collect data – Determine what information or data is available, and would be of use to help understand the current process and what key elements affect the process. The problem and goal statements in the charter provide a good start for this conversation. Documented issues and the process map may also provide good insights. This is always a tricky part of the project. An experienced LSS facilitator is a great asset at this point.

  c. ANALYZE:

    i. Review the current process map – Analyze each step for value, or circle problem areas.

A common way to do this is called "value analysis". The facilitator walks team members through the individual steps of the process map. If a step meets set criteria to be deemed "value added", then it is annotated, often with the color green. If a step does not meet the set criteria, then it is often colored red. Most likely all red steps cannot be removed. But, ideally the red steps can be reduced or minimized. This is a simple and visual way to remove waste from a process.

ii. Analyze data – Once data is collected, rely on experienced LSS facilitator to provide support. Analysis is often very simple, and involves viewing the data in a variety of ways to see what is affecting the primary metric of interest. A simple graphic(s) may also be helpful (run chart, pie chart, bar chart).

iii. Conduct root cause analysis – Using Ishikawa/Fishbone diagram or "Five Why's" technique, or another method, determine the root causes of top issues. Top issues can be selected from charter, issues list, process map, and/or data analysis. Once root causes are identified, I like to start the discussion of potential solutions for each.

d. IMPROVE:

i. Develop and vet potential solutions – Document solutions in detail: include the solution, detailed notes, who will finalize development, any documents, samples or templates that are needed, who is responsible to implement the solution, when it will be implemented, benefits of the solution, and a potential metric to ensure that desired results are achieved. I prefer to

> document all of this in the form of a table. A sample of my recommendations table is provided in the following chapter.

    ii. Develop future process map – Based on recommended solutions and current process map analysis, develop a new and improved process map with duplication, rework loops, and waste removed.

    iii. Pilot or try out the new process and solutions – A trial run is a must. Pilot the solutions by either testing the new process with a segment of the organization or for a limited amount of time. Allow for feedback and adjustments. This has multiple benefits including further process improvement, and buy-in by process workers.

    iv. Adjust based on pilot feedback and findings – Return to project documentation and make adjustments as identified during the pilot period.

    v. Develop written guidance and train personnel to follow the new process – A process that isn't documented can't be adhered to. People need written guidance and training in order to understand and maintain a standard process.

e. CONTROL:

    i. Develop control plan – This is a simple tool identifying a few metrics to monitor long-term results. Always remember, too many metrics become overwhelming and the control plan is then set aside because the value is not worth the effort. The control plan should become a useful tool for the process owner, helping him or her to keep quantitative data over time to understand the health of the process.

ii. Report results – A standard reporting mechanism is helpful, as described earlier in this book. Templates for reporting allow an organization to combine individual results to show overall program success. They make reporting to stakeholders easier, with familiar formatting and content. Another way to report results is to make them visible. A hallway with project summaries printed on poster-sized displays, or a visual graphic located in a prominent area may do the trick to general interest and help maintain planned results.

iii. Implement control plan – A control plan is only of use if it is used! This tool is actually a win-win. It helps the team document results, providing simple before and after comparisons. It helps the process owner manage the process long-term, showing trends, and providing a mechanism to identify and respond to process changes.

iv. Finalize project documentation and make information available to the organization. An on-line clearinghouse or management system is invaluable for disseminating information across the organization, managing results, and keeping track of projects and people.

v. Bring team back together and confirm results – At the conclusion of the project, the process owner and LSS facilitator should sit down and discuss the appropriate timing to re-convene the team in order to review status of the process and ensure that desired results have been achieved and maintained. Just like the cleaned-up garage at home, if it's not managed and monitored, it ultimately becomes a messy garage again (this is particularly true at my house!).

7) Homework is a must. Honestly, don't you just hate sitting through a meeting where the person who called the meeting makes sure to keep everyone at the table until the entire meeting time has passed, then no actions are assigned, and you feel like the information could have just as easily been passed via an email? Is it just me? Anyhow, actions and tasks for team members are critical. "Homework" assignments outside of the project team meeting have several benefits: they help the project proceed more quickly, they create an increased sense of ownership of the project and results by team members, and there are some things that are best done by an individual with team review afterward. During the project, at the conclusion of each team meeting, actions or tasks should be identified and assigned, along with due dates. This can be in the form of a list, identifying the action to be taken, who is responsible, when action is due, and status of action. I prefer to keep this information clearly documented on the wall of the meeting room (big surprise!) for two reasons: (1) assignments are clearly documented and visible to the team, and (2) status encourages team members to get their work done. *Facilitator note: It's a bit embarrassing to see your name in bold letters displayed on a wall when you haven't come through with your task on time. This is a way to encourage everyone to do their part, and do it on time.*

8) For simply scoped projects, with an experienced facilitator, teams can expect to meet for approximately twenty to thirty hours in order to complete the entire DMAIC project approach. How this is accomplished depends on the situation. Some teams meet for an entire week and exit the week with a plan in place to pilot the recommendations. Other teams meet two mornings a week over several weeks. Both scenarios work fine. *A word of caution: Don't meet for less than two hours at a time – single hour meetings don't gain enough momentum, don't allow for enough progress, and too much of the time is spent starting the meeting and bringing participants up-*

to-speed from the prior meeting. Also, one meeting per week may not be enough – the team will take longer to progress and everyone knows that the longer a project lingers, the greater the chance of failure.

9) Document all team activities. I am not a fan of meeting notes. Sometimes they are necessary, but I rarely find that the value associated with documenting discussions in paragraph format is worth the effort. This medium for information sharing in LSS is not as useful as keeping track of all exercises and results. So, what is a good facilitator to do? I have found that a simple excel file with a tab and worksheet dedicated to each tool is a great way to keep organized. I call this the "project file". There is no need for a dozen separate files that are difficult to manage and track. A single project file is part of my keeping-it-simple approach. The worksheets are placed in chronological order, so the file also serves as a guide for the facilitator. An added bonus is that there is no need for meeting minutes (Yay! Did I mention that I loathe typing up meeting minutes?), because if you update your project file after each team meeting, then all of the activities are documented – no need to duplicate the effort by creating separate meeting minutes. Also, as a standard part of documenting team meetings, I always walk around the room and take a picture of each flip chart sheet or white board that has been used during the meeting. The pictures can then be used for multiple purposes: documentation, reference, or back up when that white board is invariably erased. Some of the project steps and tools can be documented by pasting a picture onto the appropriate worksheet in the excel file. Other steps and tools can be typed up as a table or graphic to be used in briefing or training materials at the conclusion of the project. A picture of the project file is provided in the following chapter.

There you have it: the streamlined recipe for running a LSS project. This may seem like a lot for the new-comer, but I guarantee that many Lean Six Sigma experts who read this book will have plenty of head nods and head shakes when it comes to this section. This approach may seem too simple for some, but like I said, I have found that this streamlined approach works well. With a little experience, it can become second nature. No need for a four-year industrial engineering degree (which I have, so I feel that I can personally make this statement), or a master's degree with a global emphasis on best business practices (which I have, so again I feel that I can make this statement). I tell my students and mentees that with this approach they can improve processes wherever they go, and can become invaluable to any organization, FOR THE REST OF THEIR LIVES! What a deal.

Good Results to Amazing Results ("Replication")

If your work involves administration, logistics, or production in your organization, chances are that you are not the only one involved with administration, logistics, or production. So, once you have your process squared away (waste has been removed, activities and tools have been standardized, you are the local super hero of administration, logistics, or production), will you keep your solutions a secret? Let's hope not.

At a minimum, once a Lean Six Sigma project is complete, leadership is briefed on the results. And, typically, while the excitement of these fantastic results is fresh, you will be compelled to share your joy with friends, family, and co-workers.

Telling others is a natural human response, which is good. But, there are amazing possibilities that have been missed. Consider if you will:

You are a member of a team that orders parts for one of the organization's product lines. Your team has reduced parts order time from fourteen days to twenty-four hours via a Lean Six Sigma project. This has resulted in:

- Reduction of required warehouse storage space from 2000 to 1000 square feet
- Reduction in overall production cycle time from 20 to 10 days
- Reduction in manpower requirements from 3 full-time equivalents (FTE's) to 1 FTE
- All of this is calculated to represent a cost savings of $500,000 per year

Fantastic! Tell your friends, family, and co-workers!

Now, think about the other parts order teams that support the rest of the organization's product lines. Perhaps we are talking about ten other lines and teams. What would happen if you shared (or management directed the rest to use) your new methods? Granted, it may not be a direct plug and play situation. The other teams may need to make adjustments based on different constraints or circumstances. But, ultimately if they use the new methods that your team developed, you could potentially multiply your results by ten!! While most of us would call this a duplication opportunity, we've opted for a trendier word: REPLICATION. Sounds nifty, right? But even better than the opportunity to use a trendy word, think of the possible results:

- Suddenly the cost savings of $500,000 per year turns into $5,000,000 per year (or some other amount that is significantly greater than the original $500,000)

Now, you truly are a super hero. Tell your friends, family, and co-workers! (And possibly negotiate a raise!)

The moral here is that most likely whatever you have improved, there is someone else doing something similar that can be improved using your team's solutions. Streamline your streamlining. Imagine the possibilities. DON'T FORGET TO LOOK FOR OPPORTUNITIES TO REPLICATE.

Replication isn't limited to identical processes or responsibilities. After all, fast food restaurants have been known to benchmark with NASCAR pit crews to find faster ways to serve customers. Representatives from a Marine Corps base in California visited a local university to compare notes and look for better ways to maintain facilities and grounds. Your team may be able to identify great opportunities to replicate results in less than obvious ways. Open your minds and let the creativity flow.

Setbacks and Setback Instigators

Up until this point, I have been guilty of painting a fairly rose-colored picture of Lean Six Sigma program introduction, establishment, and management. The word "simple" has been used 21 times so far in the book – truly, I counted.

Is starting a Lean Six Sigma program all sunshine and rainbows? Well, of course not, silly! It takes hard work, dedication, thick skin, and an enduring drive. People who are unfamiliar with the term Lean Six Sigma, or the concepts of removing waste, standardizing processes, and meeting customer requirements, often push back when approached. There are many negative responses. But, for those who choose to engage, if they follow the path without too many diversions, they will reap real and measurable benefits. I have often stated that working "in the field" with Marines, out with the regiments and battalions, and getting to measurable results quickly is like a vitamin shot in the arm – instantly energizing and revitalizing. These many quick wins and happy Marines make it easy to return to those who reject the concepts at first. Also, there is no better marketing plan than success. If we can help a regiment save time or money or reduce defects by using Lean Six Sigma, the positively affected Marines tell others. Plus, we can use real examples that are understandable and hit close to home, when presenting or providing training. Standing at the shore, another wave of interest rolls in, and suddenly we are receiving more word-of-mouth requests for training and support. This has been a true exponential growth model. Here we are in the eighth year of Lean Six Sigma in the Marine Corps (13th year, actually, if we include the infancy stages while sampling process improvement tools to find the best fit), demand is not dying down, but continues to increase: our classes have wait lists months ahead of the training date, we have new groups contacting us on a continuing basis requesting more information or support. You can experience the same sort of growth and continuing interest in your organization, as long as you persevere through or avoid setbacks.

Let's talk about common setbacks (or causes of setbacks), along with potential solutions. I have personally seen several of these. Fortunately, Lean Six Sigma provides measurable results, and quickly. This makes the setbacks easier to manage.

Lean to the Corps

Setback 1: Initial Lack of Buy-In
- Problem – Leaders are not engaged, or the "frozen" middle management prevents the initial leadership message from getting to the working level. This could be due to lack of familiarity, bad personal experiences, or just plain cantankerous personalities.
- Solution – The message throughout this book is success. There is no better marketer. If people see successful results from Lean Six Sigma work, or see that by participating, their path to success or promotion improves, then the frozen middle will melt. If leaders can understand how process improvement will benefit them, then they will engage. Proof of concept with real results is the best response to this setback. As a side note, I mentioned earlier that we are a team of about fifteen people, supporting hundreds of thousands of Marines. So, in our experience, when we encounter lack of buy-in, we usually move on to another group who is awaiting support. Those who weren't interested can often become interested when they see others use the tools. We can always circle back around to support the organization once they decide that they are interested in trying Lean Six Sigma.

Setback 2: Starting Without the Basics
- Problem - Once people's eyes are opened to the possibilities associated with Lean Six Sigma, they often take off running: *It's so exciting, why wait?!? The sooner we can start the better. I've read "Lean to the Corps"! Good to go! No need to worry about planning, templates, software, and experienced help.* This reminds me of a time that I gave parenting advice to friends prior to having any children of my own, but I had watched an hour long special on television, so I was ready to advise. Later, after I actually had my own children, I realized how ridiculous my advice had been. A one-hour documentary did not give me the basics I needed to understand parenting. Just like a

short book or introductory class for Lean Six Sigma will not prepare you to start a Lean Six Sigma project or program.

- Solution – Go back to the "Getting Started" section of this book. Review the recommended steps. Make sure to pull in some experienced help. If the first source of guidance doesn't feel right, maybe you need to try a second source. Instincts are often correct. Even without real Lean Six Sigma experience under your belt, you can probably pick out the fake "experts" in the field.

Setback 3: Changes in Leadership

- Problem - You've got everyone trained and aligned, and then the big boss leaves! Whether you are working in a transient environment (like the military) or not, sometimes there is a changing of the guard. The incoming leader(s) may want to create a legacy, which he or she believes must be unique or different from the last guy. Must the change include moving away from Lean Six Sigma?
- Solution – Build your foundation on solid ground, and make Lean Six Sigma a part of the culture and general management practices of the organization. This means including LSS in strategic planning, long-term measurement and management. Make it the go-to toolset for any process problems, with the standard response by staff based on common LSS practices. This way, if an incoming leader wants to make a change, the organization will respond by using LSS to support that change.
- A secondary benefit of adopting Lean Six Sigma is the proven track record of the toolset. LSS is a common practice in both public and private sectors. Incoming leadership may already be familiar with LSS, either academically or from personal experience.

Setback 4: Changes in Personnel

Lean to the Corps

- Problem - What if the boss is still around, but your trained workers move?
- Solution – This actually isn't a problem, it's normal. A Lean Six Sigma program should be developed with turnover in mind. A training plan includes continual training. Keep the majority of staff (or 100%, if possible!) trained at the LSS Yellow Belt level. Provide LSS Green Belt training at a logical frequency – perhaps quarterly or twice each year. Make LSS Black Belt training available to those who have a proven track record as Green Belts. Treat it as a goal and a reward for a job well done. Include Lean Six Sigma activity and growth as a part of performance evaluations or promotions.

Setback 5: Over-Complication

- Problem – Have you ever noticed that the first season of a good drama or comedy show has a crisp story line and characters who are easy to get to know and understand? Then by season four or five, the story line is complex, characters have come and gone, and it's just not as fun to watch anymore (yes, I am talking about Heroes and Homeland and Game of Thrones!)? Growth of complexity over time is a natural, and perhaps necessary, path. The problem is that when it comes to Lean Six Sigma, complication and complexity are the opposite of what we are trying to achieve. If we make it too hard for people to get started, or leaders to manage, or training to be scheduled, we are simply killing the program from friendly fire.
- Solution – Keep your eye on the ball. Review the program on a regular basis for ease of involvement, understanding, and use. Balance maturity of the program (standardization, templates, and training) with a goal to remain simple and pure. Remember, good may detract from great (thank you, Mr. Collins for that

insight[22]), and you should always seek to make joining the LSS bandwagon the preferential choice to the status quo.

Setback 6: Mistaking Inflexible for Standardized
- Problem – A problem on the other end of the spectrum of complexity is becoming inflexible, in the name of standardization. The explanation may be: "The Lean Six Sigma approach can't be flexible or responsive to varying needs, because we have standardized our approach." This is wrong. Do not accept this explanation.
- Solution – This problem usually only occurs with people who are new to Lean Six Sigma, or managers who try to manage a LSS program, but don't have any field experience of actually running a project and improving processes. This is not usually an area of difficulty with experienced practitioners. Continuous improvement is all about continuing to get better, i.e. CHANGE.

Setback 7: Competing Programs
- Problem – What if LSS is cropping up from other sources in the organization, and not following the standardized strategic approach; or what if rogue personnel engage in process improvement that isn't LSS?!!
- Solution – It's all good… don't worry, be friendly. If your organization is large enough that Lean Six Sigma is showing up in various forms, and it was not planned by your LSS program office, simply go on a fact-finding search. Get to know who is using LSS and how they got started. Let them know that there is an overall strategy for the organization and bring them into the strategy. If there are other process improvement efforts that are going on during your LSS work, go on a fact-finding search (sound familiar?). Find out what is going on, and how it started. I'm

---

[22] Yet another reference to one of my favorite books!

willing to bet that your organization has room for other process improvement work. As long as there isn't direct conflict with planned processes and projects, incorporate their results into your overall visibility of process improvement. If a manager of a process that is in the middle of a LSS project wants to try another route, recommend delay until the team has concluded, to prevent confusion. But, honestly, all true process improvement is good. No need to feel threatened or push back on other good things. Invite them to join the club. Share information. Create visibility of good results.

Setback 8: Inexperience
- Problem – One person has had LSS Green Belt training, so we are ready to start a LSS program now, right?
- Solution – Well, you can possibly get to some good results from a single project or two, but starting a program will be a bumpy road with wasted time and possibly some missteps that could be easily avoided with experienced guidance. An experienced LSS Master Black Belt, or even Black Belt, brings samples, examples, templates, lessons learned, streamlined approaches, and planning experience that a newer LSS practitioner won't yet have. Even if you must bring in contracted support, do so. At least for the first few months or until you can hire your own experienced practitioner. It will take at least a year or two for your newly trained LSS Green Belt to gain enough experience to lead a LSS program – and that's an optimistic timeframe. When it comes to experience, nothing beats experience. There are no short cuts.

Setback 9: Arrogance
- Problem – In the Lean Six Sigma world, there are many intelligent and highly educated people. When working with engineers, scientists, or humans for that

matter, there may be some bad apples. These are the experts who like to be treated as royalty. You know the type: when they arrive, they expect other people to adjust schedules in order to accommodate their needs. A bit of ooo-ing and aaah-ing in their presence is always welcome. Arrogance is an immediate turn-off in any environment, and is certainly not appreciated in the Marine Corps.

- Solution – First of all, there is no room in Lean Six Sigma for arrogance. Everyone rolls up their sleeves and works side-by-side for the benefit of the organization. A true intelligent person has not only book smarts, but also communication smarts. He or she can read the room by assessing non-spoken cues, in addition to spoken cues – and can respond accordingly. The best intelligent people can relate to anyone at any level (even statisticians!). They can speak in a way that is understood by everyone in the room, and can easily transition between the languages of mathematics, analyses, and daily process management. They are gracious in that they can make anyone feel comfortable. Make sure you hire or promote true intelligent people, who can help your program succeed by turning people on instead of off, and backing it up with true experience and know-how.

Setback 10: Shelf-Life
- Problem – So, your LSS program has been around a while, now everyone is itching to move on to something else. After all, we've always done it that way! (I can't believe I've gotten this far in the book and this is only the second time I've referred to that phrase that I hear so often… in so many contexts.)
- Solution – Actually, if your program is running like a well-oiled machine: top problem areas identified, teams assigned, teams trained, process improved, results monitored and reported to management team, then focus moves to next problem areas, teams assigned, teams trained…. With review of mission,

vision, customer requirements, gaps and headaches (see "Top Down vs. Bottom Up discussion earlier in this book), ultimately updating the queue of projects every 6 to 12 months, this should become just a part of the way you do business. Better tools and templates may come along, but the basic Lean Six Sigma approach is founded on the scientific method. This has withstood the test of time. Remember, with Lean Six Sigma there is not a need to move on to other approaches, but rather keep the approach and just get better at implementing it.

Continuing Growth

Come on, are we really trying to say that Lean Six Sigma should not only become a part of the very fabric of an organization, but should continue to grow? Well, yes.

With the combination of demand for this skill across all industries, rapid results, and benefits to both organization and individuals, this program becomes self-perpetuating... as long as leadership, rewards, promotions, training, projects, results, and controls are all working together. (And, the program isn't inhibited by well intentioned - or poorly intentioned - souls who block progress.) Sounds a lot like capitalism! Works well on its own until tampered with by over-regulation and self-inflicted wounds. Sounds a lot like America! A perfect fit.

As Abraham Lincoln once said, "...if destruction be our lot we must ourselves be its author and finisher. As a nation of free men, we will live forever or die by suicide."

Your Lean Six Sigma program will live forever... or die by suicide.

PART 4. A BIT OF HOW-TO: THE REAL DEAL, WITH EXAMPLES

– "With [Lean Six Sigma], the reward is not for effort, the reward is for results."

Harry Jackson, LSS Master Black Belt

Streamlined Lean Six Sigma Project Tools

Nothing tells the story of process improvement better than actual stories of process improvement! With this in mind, our chapter here is dedicated to real projects that have been conducted, using the streamlined approach to LSS described in chapter three. Note that all of these processes followed the same Define-Measure-Analyze-Improve-Control approach. Though the processes vary significantly (we can all agree that maintaining a vehicle is very different from physical fitness tracking for those who don't meet height and weight standards); they are all processes, and, thus, can be addressed using the same process improvement methodology.

Before we look at project examples, let's take a closer look at common project deliverables using the streamlined Lean Six Sigma approach. Please note that while these are common elements of streamlined projects, the team facilitator may choose to use alternate or additional tools. I am simply reviewing some of the tools that I commonly use. There are many others. Consider this the chicken stock for your soup. You may add your favorite vegetables and spices to your liking. Just don't over-do it. The prettiest graphics and diagrams can make a facilitator look like a statistics virtuoso, but if these pretty pictures don't contribute to the results of the project, then by creating them, you have just wasted the time of all team members (and some team members will recognize that time has been wasted, which may turn them against Lean Six Sigma, which could have a detrimental effect on your entire program). So, keep your eye on the prize: results.

a. DMAIC

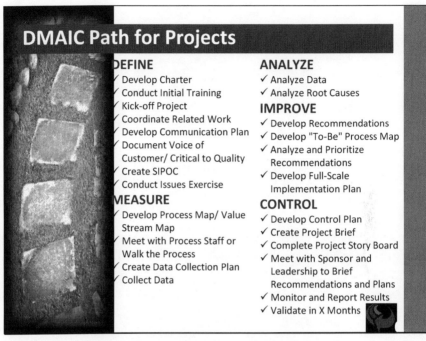

DMAIC Path for Projects

DEFINE
- ✓ Develop Charter
- ✓ Conduct Initial Training
- ✓ Kick-off Project
- ✓ Coordinate Related Work
- ✓ Develop Communication Plan
- ✓ Document Voice of Customer/ Critical to Quality
- ✓ Create SIPOC
- ✓ Conduct Issues Exercise

MEASURE
- ✓ Develop Process Map/ Value Stream Map
- ✓ Meet with Process Staff or Walk the Process
- ✓ Create Data Collection Plan
- ✓ Collect Data

ANALYZE
- ✓ Analyze Data
- ✓ Analyze Root Causes

IMPROVE
- ✓ Develop Recommendations
- ✓ Develop "To-Be" Process Map
- ✓ Analyze and Prioritize Recommendations
- ✓ Develop Full-Scale Implementation Plan

CONTROL
- ✓ Develop Control Plan
- ✓ Create Project Brief
- ✓ Complete Project Story Board
- ✓ Meet with Sponsor and Leadership to Brief Recommendations and Plans
- ✓ Monitor and Report Results
- ✓ Validate in X Months

Figure 5 Streamlined DMAIC Path for Projects

The next several pictures and comments are from my meeting guidance files. These serve as an overview of streamlined LSS meeting activities. I'm including pictures so that you can more easily understand the concepts. Sensitive content has been removed.

Lean to the Corps

b. HOW TO ORGANIZE IT ALL:

Over the years, I have created a standard "project file" using Microsoft Excel. My reasoning isn't that Excel is the best or only option for documenting projects, but rather, that multiple worksheets per file, with labeled tabs, seem to lend themselves well to organizing all of the deliverables associated with a Lean Six Sigma project. The tabs are organized in chronological order, to follow the simple step-by-step approach that I typically use when applying DMAIC to a process. The figure below provides a screen shot of my standard project file in Excel:

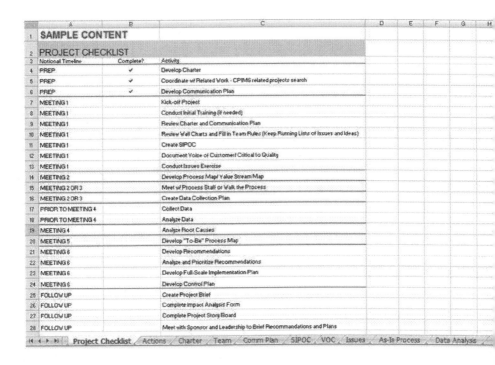

Figure 6 Project File Using MSExcel

c. MEETING BASICS:

I purposely use hand-written flip chart paper (self-adhesive) placed in an easily visible location in the meeting space. By the way, a meeting space can be anywhere with vertical surfaces: meeting room, office, warehouse (yes, you can even tape paper to chain-link fence), vehicle maintenance bay… you get the picture.

While all of this paper on the walls may look a bit juvenile (I always state up front, and without apologies, that the room may end up looking like a kindergarten classroom), I have found that this is the most efficient way to run project meetings. Don't let anyone talk you into conducting the meeting by projecting an electronic file on a screen. I repeat, DON'T PROJECT A FILE ON A SCREEN as the standard way to run your meeting. Sure, there are exceptions: if you have a data file to review, or want to view a brief that has been developed, that sort of thing. When you run your project meetings by documenting what you are doing on-screen, I guarantee (trust me, I have collected data on this) that the discussion will turn to formatting, fixing typos, and before you know it, you have lost focus from your current exercise or tool. Plus, you can only project one thing at a time. What if you need to view earlier tools to support the current discussion or action? Can't do it if you are projecting on a screen. Wall charts are the best.

When using flip chart paper or butcher paper on a wall, don't worry, if you keep a roll of blue painter's tape handy you can secure that paper to just about anything: over existing hanging pictures, doors, wardrobes, fencing (as mentioned above). And, if you use blue tape (it must be good blue tape, not the cheap fake stuff, I learned this the hard way), you will be able to remove your meeting artifacts from the walls with no damage to anything beneath.

Use thick markers, no fine tips. And make sure those markers don't bleed through your paper. You may be banished from the space forever if you mark-up someone's walls.

Why the office supplies lesson? The answer is simple: if you have the right tools that keep meeting activities visible and ease the transition from one task to the next, then you will have a much better chance of succeeding overall with your project goals. By sitting at the head of a table to run a team meeting, and documenting your discussion and activities on a piece of paper in front of you, *where no one else can see what you are writing*, you give your team permission to check out and not participate. You cheat them out of the education and skills they could be gaining in order to go out and improve processes on their own. You don't give them an opportunity to see what you are writing and possibly clarify or correct if you have misunderstood what they have said. You allow the team to meander and get off topic. I could go on.

Okay, now that some of the basics have been covered, let's talk about project tools and activities. At this point, some of you may be asking, "Wasn't this covered in chapter three?" Actually, yes. But these explanations are a bit more detailed, and there is something to be said about repetition and learning. Plus, you and I both know that there are skimmers in this world who will skip over the meat of this book to get to the examples chapter, so we are helping them out by providing a quick introduction to the tools. This is by no means a complete description of Lean Six Sigma tools. I am simply providing dialogue and guidance to supplement formal training and texts.

d. CHARTER:

The charter is the team's guiding document. In one to two pages, it states the problem to be solved, goals, scope of the project, team members, timeline, and other pertinent information needed to get started. This is typically drafted prior to the first team meeting. In my experience, it is best for the team facilitator (LSS Green Belt, Black Belt, or Master Black Belt, depending on the complexity of the project) to draft this with the process owner. During the charter drafting meeting, the team members and timeline will be determined. It's best if the process owner, who is usually someone in a position of authority, contacts the team members individually to tell them they have been selected to participate and why. This sets the tone for the team: this project is important, it's important to leadership, team members have been selected because they have knowledge or skills that are needed. It's also a good idea for the process owner to attend the first few minutes of the first meeting (and then sit in on occasion during future meetings) to repeat the message: this is important.

e. MEETING CHECKLIST:

This serves as your team meeting agenda as well as a visual representation of team progress. I don't know about you, but I truly enjoy checking a box when I have completed a task. This is why there is always a box to the left of all of my meeting checklist items. Sometimes team members beat me to it, and check the box. No problem, consider it a gift. Everyone feels better when they check a box.

The meeting checklist saves the facilitator from having to sit down and dream up the next meeting agenda. Simply pick up where you left off, and plan for what you think you may be able to accomplish with your given amount of meeting time – make sure you brush up on any tools or tasks that may be rusty or unfamiliar – even practice possible team scenarios to make sure you are prepared.

In addition, the team now has a visual of progress after each meeting. No need to wonder if there is a light at the end of the tunnel. A full map of the tunnel is on the wall during each and every team meeting, with those lovely boxes checked and serving as proof of progress. I'll even share with you a little secret about my list: the first several items are quick and can be accomplished during the first team meeting. Why does this matter? The team then sees real progress right away (there's something about quick wins and feelings of accomplishment that keep everyone positive and productive). Then it's not so painful if data collection and analysis take longer than expected. And for some reason, data collection and analysis often take longer than expected.

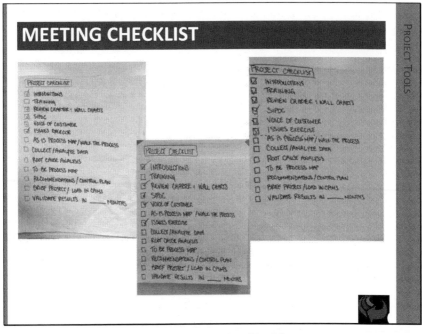

Figure 7 Sample Meeting Checklists

f. ISSUES EXERCISE:

The "Issues Exercise" is usually the third or fourth tool that the team uses along the DMAIC path. I'm opting to explain it first because the facilitator should begin to document issues and problems with the process from the first moments of the first meeting. You see, team members are typically subject matter experts for the process that is being improved. They work with the process, possibly daily. They will come to the first meeting ready, willing, and able to describe the many things that are wrong with the process (we call these "issues") and will also gladly tell you how to fix many of those things (we call these "ideas"). A seasoned facilitator will be able to hear the stated issues and ideas easily throughout meeting conversations. I prefer to silently walk over to our issues and ideas lists and simply add the stated item to the lists each time I hear an issue or an idea. It's important to keep the team moving and following the established agenda (from the meeting checklist, with boxes that can be checked- you are welcome!), so when team members observe that their issues and ideas have been documented for all to see, they know that those items will not be forgotten. Then the facilitator can easily sway the team back to the work at hand. This is also of benefit to the facilitator who will use the starter list of issues to build on when it is actually time to conduct the issues exercise task. When conducting the task, simply bring the team's attention to the list of issues, which should be written on chart paper, hanging on the wall. State that the list serves as a start to informally identifying what is currently wrong with the process. Brainstorm with the team to capture additional issues. After brainstorming, the team then votes and prioritizes the sometimes-lengthy list of issues. The plan is then for top issues to be addressed during the course of the project. Usually when top issues are resolved, many of the lesser issues are automatically resolved as well. Note that sometimes the team charter must be revised because the original problem statement isn't quite right, after digging into process issues.

ISSUES EXERCISE

	Issue	Primary
1	Competing priorities of a maintenance shop	5
2		1
3		1
4		1
5		1
6		5
7	Lack of maintenance validations	0
8		3
9		5
10	Parts take too long to arrive	●
11		0
12		6
13		3
14		1
15	No money to buy parts	2

PROJECT TOOLS

Figure 8 Issues Exercise (sensitive content has been covered)

g. SIPOC:

The name of this strange sounding tool is an acronym that stands for Suppliers – Inputs – Process – Outputs – Customers. I have not always used the SIPOC. Early in my career, I thought it sounded odd, and was redundant – after all, the team would be documenting the process during the process mapping phase of the project. But now I am a strong proponent of the SIPOC. Its true value, as I've seen, is to establish a foundation to help the team understand the process. Many times, we will have team members who are experts in one part of the process or another, but not the entire process. Sometimes team members have no idea what occurs before or after their part of the process. Conducting the SIPOC exercise during the first or at the latest, the second, meeting is invaluable. The SIPOC serves as a neatly wrapped summary of the process. It can be created quickly, generating a sense of understanding, accomplishment, and team work right away.

When generating a SIPOC, I prefer to work from the right to left by having the team members first identify who is using the outputs of the process. These "end users" are also known as "Customers" of the process. Once the customers are identified, then the Outputs that they receive are easily listed. From there, a very high-level Process (6-12 steps max!) is documented so that it is clear where the process begins and ends with a few key steps in between (this is a visual representation of the "scope" of the project). From there, conversation easily flows to what is needed in order to conduct the process. These are the Inputs. The simple next step is to list who provides each of the inputs, the Suppliers. At the end of the conversation, you have a SIPOC, visible for all. And a clear summary of what is being addressed by the project. If the team takes longer than ten to twenty minutes to conduct this exercise, then it was not facilitated correctly. This should be a quick, high level, low granularity (consultants love that word) effort. The value is that it builds team understanding, and everyone starts with the same foundation.

SIPOC – Process Summary

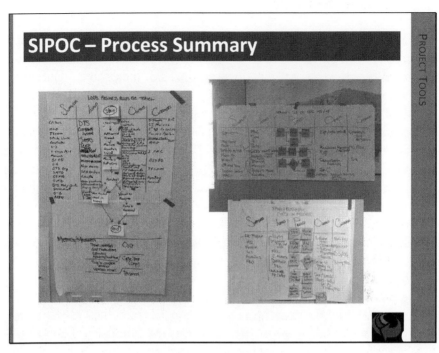

Figure 9 Sample SIPOC's

h. "AS-IS" OR CURRENT PROCESS MAP:

If you do NOTHING ELSE, map the process. Recall from chapter 3, a process map is a visual representation of the steps of a process, much like a flow chart. This is an eye-opening activity. Team members nearly always say, "I didn't know we do it that way.", or "Why do we do it that way?" When facilitating this exercise, I am always reminded of flight attendants. You know, the ones who relay the same message in many different ways as people are exiting the airplane (good-bye, have a nice day, good-bye, enjoy your afternoon, hope you enjoyed the flight, good-bye…). Your job during this exercise will be to ask "What happens next?", "And then what?": the same thing over and over until you've mapped out the process from first step to last. A word to the wise: listen for the word "should". When you hear that word, then your team has transitioned to improving the process. They are no longer identifying the current way the process is conducted, but are instead talking about a better way, or the official way the process is expected to run. But, during the current state process mapping exercise, the team is documenting what <u>is actually happening now</u>, not what they would like to see in the future. Even if activities

69

don't match standard procedures or rules, make sure to capture what is actually happening, the current way the process is running.

Why do I say, if you do nothing else, map the process? In my experience, when a team sees a process visually, and documents current methods, they can't help but notice problem areas. At a minimum, the team will find a couple of areas to improve. Sometimes the map will help the team realize that there is a need to standardize, because multiple approaches for the same process have been documented. When a team says, "we don't have a process", that typically means that they just have many ways of conducting the process. In this case, I usually guide the team to map the two or three most common ways that the process is conducted. This creates a visual that helps the team to identify best practices from each approach, which will help later on when it is time to develop the new process (or the team may opt to scrap the whole thing and start over – it's always an interesting experience).

When creating the process map, ALWAYS use sticky notes. If possible, roll out a large strip or strips of butcher paper to create a working space on a wall, visible to all team members (white boards can be used, too, but I prefer butcher paper that can be rolled up and transported). NEVER draw the process step boxes with a marker on your butcher paper (and you know how I feel about projecting an electronic version on the screen while building the process – DON'T). When you are mapping the process, it never fails, at some point a team member will realize that a step was missed or the order isn't quite right. If you are using sticky notes, no problem! If you have drawn the process step boxes with a marker, you have a problem.

I also like to use multiple colors of notes to represent different things. The colors matter not, as long as you have a key (see box in top right corner of picture below). In the example, green represents process steps, orange represents time related notes, blue identifies who is conducting the step, and pink lists tools or forms used for the task.

Once the process is mapped, a value analysis can be conducted, identifying each step as "value-added" or "non-value-added". If value analysis doesn't seem to fit the situation, another option is to simply circle problem areas with a nice, big, thick marker.

"AS-IS" or Current Process

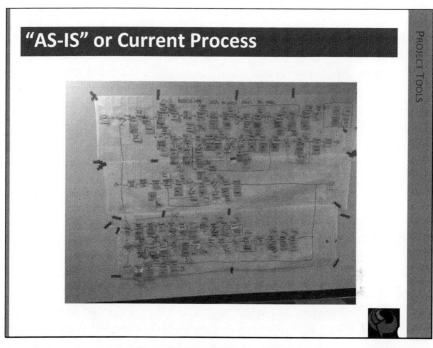

Figure 10 Sample Process Map

i. DATA COLLECTION AND ANALYSIS:

You project is chugging along. All team members have become fast friends. You have led the group through the first few exercises without a hitch and are feeling like the best darn facilitator ever. Now it's time to collect data. You aren't sure where to start. Once you do identify what data to collect, your team members hit road blocks. The numbers turn out to be incorrect or much more difficult to collect than originally planned. Your team schedule is delayed. Its back to the drawing board, or the due date for data needs an extension, or the team realizes after the first round of data collection that a key milestone was missed and now you need to go back out to collect more data. You no longer feel like the best darn facilitator, and mock that naive pre-data collection version of yourself. What have you done wrong? Well, nothing really. All of this is fairly normal. With experience, the data collection phase of a project becomes less painful, and you will begin to see common roadblocks before they occur and may be able to prevent them. But, data collection is often the most difficult part of a DMAIC project. If schedules are delayed, it is usually during data collection. Forgive yourself, forgive your teammates, call on a more experienced mentor if needed, and move on.

Once you have reliable data, it serves multiple purposes: (1) data can serve as a baseline for improvement (for example, error rate reduced from 90% to 5% or cycle time improved from seven to two days), (2) it can point the team to areas that need improvement (what caused that spike in cost?; there is an increasing trend of errors; who knew that finance was sitting on the paperwork for an average of 10 days?), (3) data collection can help the team to understand whether or not the right metrics are being emphasized by the organization and if they are encouraging the right behaviors.

Warning: when it comes to data collection, make sure the juice is worth the squeeze. It is easy to fall into the trap of collecting more data or more details than what is needed. I realize that to statisticians, this concept equates to blasphemy. But, hear me out. Often, three months-worth of historical data tells the same story as a year. Sampling every 10th occurrence can direct the team to the same findings as collecting data on every occurrence. Using existing data may be as enlightening as collecting new data. Determining the best quantity and source of data gets easier with experience. But, sometimes even the most experienced get it wrong. I always recommend at least a quick discussion with your mentor before settling on data collection plans.

Advice: when it comes to data analysis, keep it simple. There are great tools available for data analysis. Excel with add-ins, Minitab, SPC software, you have tons of options. The data analysis serves to guide the team. It should include creating a picture, or visual representation of the data. A table is good, but a chart or graph is much better. While a statistical summary of graphics may impress, often a simple run chart, bar chart, or pie chart can clearly tell the story of your data.

Do you like a good mystery? Team members become fine little investigators. The plot thickens, or gets more interesting (or even fun!) during data collection and analysis.

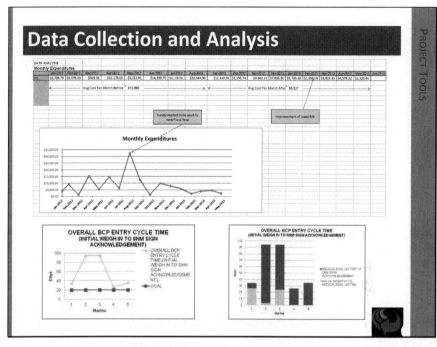

Figure 11 Sample Data Analyses

j. ROOT CAUSE ANALYSIS:

My tool of choice for root cause analysis is known as fishbone or Ishikawa[23] diagram. At this point, we are simply performing organized brainstorming. The "bones" of the fish serve as categories for the brainstorming (I like to use Man, Method, Machine, Miscellaneous). The "head" of the fish is the problem for which we are seeking root causes. I typically select the problems from Issues Exercise results, or outliers from Data Collection. For smaller scoped projects we will commonly produce up to three fishbone diagrams. When filling in the diagram, a simple approach is to ask "why?" multiple times. Team members are often more than happy to point out why the problem exists, and why the cause occurs, and why the secondary cause occurs... until the point where they don't have an answer, which is usually several levels into asking "why?". When your team runs out of

---

[23] Named after Kaoru Ishikawa, one of our "Fathers of Quality". Ishikawa was a colleague of W. Edwards Deming, referenced earlier. While known for emphasizing the seven quality tools taught in the LSS Green Belt curriculum, one of the tools is named for him.

answers (body language is pretty common here – silence, avoiding eye contact, restless movement, etc.), you have most likely reached a "root cause". As a bonus, I like to take this information rich exercise a step further, continuing the dialogue by discussing potential solutions for each root cause (remember, we also have the running "Ideas" list). In order to do this, circle and number the root causes, with a marker that is not the same color as the one used for the fishbone diagram (see pictures below). The team then discusses potential solutions for the circled root causes. We are still brainstorming, and some of the ideas may be way out there, but just let the creativity flow. The potential solutions are then listed below the diagram, and numbered in order to track back to the appropriate root cause. This documented information will be used later during the "Improve" stage of the project.

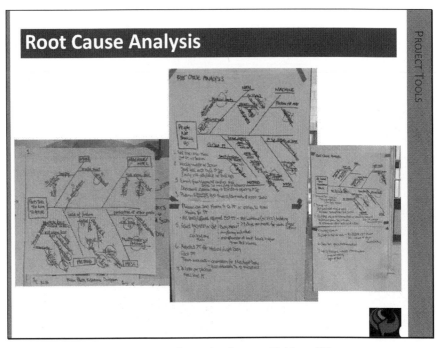

Figure 12 Sample Root Cause Analyses or Fishbone Diagrams

k. "TO-BE" OR FUTURE STATE PROCESS MAP:

By this time, the team is ready to round the corner to the true purpose of all this effort: improving the process. Much has been learned about the process. Opinions and data have been discussed, reviewed, analyzed, and possibly even debated. The team is more familiar than ever with the myths and truths of the process being addressed. Everyone is ready to get to it. Now it's time to bring in the word "should" that we didn't want to hear when we documented the original process (recall, the "As-Is" or current state process was mapped to show the original process steps prior to improvement). How *should* this new process look? What steps *should* person X take? When *should* this step take place? Most likely the team will find that the improved process has less steps or less variation than the original. Make sure to capture the improvement by summarizing: reduced process from X steps to Y steps, reduced process time from X days to Y days, reduced non-value steps from X to Y or by Z%. There are many ways to tell the story of your improved process.

Notice that the As-Is process example provided earlier was shown as a photo of the process that the team developed with sticky notes on butcher paper. The To-Be process example below is typed up as a clean electronic version of the team's process. Why is that? Well, you see the old process was just that: the old process. No need to produce a neatly typed electronic version, because it will be changing. The new process must be taught to the people in the organization and maintained by the organization. It may be included in training materials, or as an attachment to a new standard operational procedure document. So, it needs to be available in a neat and tidy electronic format.

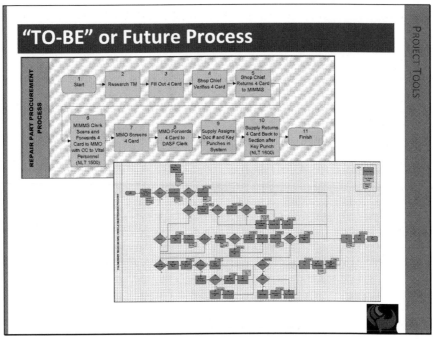

Figure 13 Future State Process Maps

1. RECOMMENDATIONS:

The preparations have been made. Now it's time to select which improvements the team will recommend. As the facilitator, you must pull everything together that has been developed so far, in order to help the team cross the finish line. Using the streamlined LSS approach, the team will have multiple sources of potential improvements to consider: the "Ideas" list, root cause analyses and draft recommendations, future state process map and anything else that may be of use when generating the team's recommendations. The table below serves as one alternative for discussing and vetting each recommendation. A fairly detailed plan can be created by documenting notes, details of what needs to be developed, who will develop each recommendation, who will implement, benefits of each recommendation, potential metrics, and timing.

Consideration should also be given to testing (or piloting) the recommendations. Piloting involves trying out a recommendation with a subset of the organization, or for a limited amount of time. If the pilot is conducted well, and expectations are managed, this allows the organization to work out any bugs in the recommendations. It also allows for feedback from employees beyond the original project team, which increases support and buy-in. After the pilot period, recommendations may be adjusted or revised based on feedback and results. The revised final recommendations can then be fully implemented.

Recommendations Details

Recommendation	Notes	Lead Team Member to develop	Details	Person to implement	Benefits	When to implement	Metrics
Standard Operating Procedure (SOP)			To-Be process, QC Checklists, Milestone checklists, Reconciliations schedules, MMO and internal training schedules, PMCS schedules		↑ Equipment readiness ↑ Capability ↑Unit O&M $ ↓Repair Cycle times		Readiness, Costs, Repair Cycle Times
Brief the commander for buy-in					Buy-in, command investment		
Train staff to new SOP			SOP, Desktop/Turnover folders		Standardization, expectation management		% of personnel trained
PMCS schedule							% of annual PMCS success
QC Checklist					Standardization, ↓ QC rejects/rework, ↓ costs, ↓ RCT		
							% of vehicles PMCS annually. Target is 100% by 31 dec 2014
Purchase hazmat kits			Spill kits, containments, safety goggles, PPE, coveralls				
Vehicle daily start-ups			Trucks, personnel		↓ Leaks ↓Replacement batteries		

Figure 14 Recommendations Details (sensitive content has been covered)

m. CONTROL PLAN:

A control plan can be anything from a simple table, providing guidance on monitoring a few key metrics, to a sturdy manual and training program with thorough content such as decision trees and guidance for responses to various scenarios. Whichever way you choose to go, ultimately the control plan should support long-term monitoring and measurement of the improved process. The plan should trigger action if improvement targets are not met or if negative trends are experienced. As we all know, it is natural for people to migrate to what is familiar, even if that means going back to the old and possibly broken way of doing things. Until the new process becomes the standard and familiar process, management needs to ensure long-term success by using some sort of control mechanism.

Control Plan

Measurement and Metrics (Control) Plan					
Recommendation	Metric	Specifications and target values	How report	Who responsible	When
Action if target not met:					

Figure 15 Simple Control Plan Template

n. WRAPPING IT UP AND IMPLEMENTING:

The team has delivered its recommendations. Everyone is feeling accomplished. Is it time to celebrate? I give you permission for a mini-celebration because you have successfully completed team requirements. But the big celebration is yet to come, after improvements are implemented and your organization is able to document concrete results. Below are a few tips for wrapping up and implementing:

- Once team completes the process improvement tasks and documentation (essentially completes the DMAIC process), finalize all documentation (I use a standard "Project File").

- Transition the information to a brief for your organization's leadership.

- Now it's time for the HARD PART... Implementing the new process and recommendations.

- Follow guidance provided in your "Recommendations Details" table.

- Pilot and adjust the new process, if this wasn't done earlier during team activities.

  - Pilot the new process with either a small group of people or for a limited period of time.

  - Collect feedback from those involved in the pilot to make any needed adjustments to the process.

- Provide the final Project File and supporting documents/information to load into a centralized repository. Any organization that is engaged in Lean Six Sigma should have a central place to document activities for others to see.

- Plan for official validation of results.

  - Convene the original team three or six months down the road to review the process and validate that planned results have been achieved.

  - Review the control plan metrics during validation and confirm that the organization is steadily monitoring results.

- Once results are validated, CELEBRATE! Celebrate the results, the team who made it possible, the organization for successfully embracing the team's recommendations, and leadership for having the insight to engage in Lean Six Sigma.

Publicly recognize those who participated. Start another project to give more people a chance to experience process improvement. Train the next group of employees. Keep the excitement and energy going. *Create or increase joy in the work place.*

o. LEAN SIX SIGMA FACILITATOR:

As the facilitator, you are the chef who pulls together a collection of ingredients to create a delectable meal, you are the artist who takes a palate of individual colors to craft a masterful portrait, you are the guide for a group of people who transform from individuals into a team that will forever have a bond beyond that of typical co-workers. They now know each other on a personal level. They may talk about families or hobbies or weekend plans. Their work environment is more enjoyable. They look forward to seeing each other (mostly). Quality of work life has improved through this endeavor. And, the primary outcome is that the process has improved.

p. EXAMPLES:

Finally! Let's see the real thing. The examples below are intended to help you, the reader, see the application of Lean Six Sigma process improvement used in many different scenarios. Please note that when conducting a project, the original Problem Statements identified in the team charter should be specific and include a quantitative description (measurements) of the situation. The examples below have been generalized to reveal the intent of the project, while excluding details that are considered confidential or sensitive in nature.

Industrial Examples

Vehicle Maintenance	
Problem to address: (from team charter)	Time for vehicles to complete all phases of maintenance needs to be reduced.

	It is unclear which phase is causing the greatest delay. Delay is affecting vehicle owners.
Issues identified during project:	• Communication with owners • Mechanic availability • Parts lead time • Training and knowledge
Root causes:	• Unclear priority communication for parts • Unclear communication for equipment • Lack of training • Inefficient quality control procedures
Recommendations:	✓ Revised process and layout ✓ Training for new process ✓ Mechanics used primarily for mechanic work, other duties dispersed among non-mechanics ✓ Consolidated Quality Control ✓ Standard review and signatures for orders ✓ Manuals made readily available at key locations
Results:	✓ Average maintenance cycle time per vehicle reduced by 35% ✓ Average number of mechanic hours per vehicle reduced by 68%

Figure 16 Vehicle Maintenance Example

Lean to the Corps

Warehouse Management	
Problem to address: (from team charter)	Warehouse spaces were recently reorganized. New procedures are not clear. Without formal methods to train incoming personnel, efficiencies gained by new layout may be lost resulting in return to less efficient operations and/or rework to achieve current results.
Issues identified during project:	• Conflicting guidance • Word-of-mouth training • Several personnel providing training • Lack of clear understanding of guiding documents and location of critical information
Root causes:	• Training authority not clearly identified • New procedures not documented • Critical reference material spread across multiple documents
Recommendations:	✓ Documented process and layout ✓ Training for new process ✓ Working binder established with standard content: Introduction, Forms, Standard Procedures w/ Pictures, List of Tools, Screen Shots, List of References, Inspection Checklists

	✓ Binders made readily available at key locations ✓ Training/Cross-Training at standard frequency
Results:	✓ All personnel cross-trained to serve as back-up for secondary positions ✓ Average supply request response time reduced and holding steady at X minutes

Figure 17 Warehouse Management Example

Inspections	
Problem to address: (from team charter)	Current inspection process has variation in inspection methods, scoring methods, inspector involvement, and cycle time. Cycle times range from X to Y days.
Issues identified during project:	• Structure of inspection teams • No dedicated inspectors • Outdated guidance • Inefficient order of inspections
Root causes:	• Traditional assignments • Varying interpretations of requirements • Lack of training • Piecemeal development of inspection procedures
Recommendations:	✓ Standardized procedures and order of inspections ✓ Inspector training

	✓ Database with automated scoring ✓ Dedicated inspectors
Results:	✓ Average inspection cycle time per organization reduced by 50% ✓ Standardized scoring ✓ Increased time available for training in low scoring areas ✓ Web-based database containing inspection results

Figure 18 Inspection Process Example

Administrative Examples

Check-In and Check-Out Process for Arriving and Departing Personnel	
Problem to address: (from team charter)	It is currently taking X days for personnel to check in and out of the organization during arrival and departure. A check sheet does exist to serve as a guide, but it includes unnecessary requirements and the order is not logical.
Issues identified during project:	• Non-essential requirements on check sheet • Order of sheet doesn't align with locations • Check sheets don't provide any office contact

	information or hours of operation
	• Records and documentation requirements are unclear
Root causes:	• Procedures developed over time, by adding stops to existing list
	• Unclear priorities from leadership
	• No standardized method across all organizations
	• Lack of communication across organizations
Recommendations:	✓ Revised process, reduced requirements, adjusted order of requirements
	✓ Provided map, points of contact, and available office hours on check list
	✓ Forwarded procedures to leadership for replication consideration
Results:	✓ Reduced number of process steps from 16 to 9
	✓ Average check in cycle time reduced by 67%
	✓ Average check out cycle time reduced by 40%

Figure 19 Check-In and Check-Out Process Example

Manning Support Process	
Problem to address: (from team charter)	Manpower support requests constantly arrive from various sources with missing or incorrect

	information. This results in last minute changes, incorrect responses, and possibly affects career opportunities for personnel.
Issues identified during project:	• Critical information missing • Exaggerated or incorrect priorities • Timeliness of requests • Duplicate requests
Root causes:	• No standard process • Requests accepted by multiple offices with varying information requirements • Lack of training • No communication of information requirements • No status updates
Recommendations:	✓ Standard format for requests ✓ Single entry point into process ✓ Missing information addressed upon receipt ✓ Point of contacts identified and distributed ✓ Criteria established for prioritization
Results:	✓ Reduced error rate of request documentation to < 5% ✓ Average response time reduced by 40%

Figure 20 Manning Support Process Example

Body Composition Program for Maintaining Height and Weight Standards	
Problem to address: (from team charter)	It currently takes X months to process personnel into the official Body Composition Program when height and weight standards are not met. This results in re-work due to expiring lab tests and affects time to return personnel to within standards.
Issues identified during project:	• Competing priorities • Varying documentation requirements by organizations • Forms and information files not standardized • Expiring lab work • No standard physical or nutritional guidelines
Root causes:	• No pre-requisites or training for coordinators • Guidance is not specific • No standard formats for documentation • Nutritional guidance is not officially addressed • Responsibilities/ authority unclear
Recommendations:	✓ Revised process ✓ Detailed guidance published ✓ Training for new process ✓ Standard folder format with sample content ✓ Coordinated physical and nutritional training

Lean to the Corps

	✓ Specific authority designated ✓ Training for coordinators developed and provided within X days of assignment
Results:	✓ Reduced processing time by 60% ✓ Reduced rework due to expiring lab work to 0

Figure 21 Body Composition Program Example

Logistics Examples

Field Operations Setup	
Problem to address: (from team charter)	Time to setup for field operations takes X hours. This requires a quantity of Y personnel to be engaged for Z% of the work day.
Issues identified during project:	• Procedures vary each time • Lacking accountability • Unclear assignments of responsibility • Vehicles not in order of required activity
Root causes:	• People are untrained • No standard methods • Personnel are always different • No written policy • No centralized control

Recommendations:	✓ Standard procedures with positions and responsibilities documented ✓ Training for new process ✓ Consistent personnel and driver assignments ✓ Turnover training for incoming personnel
Results:	✓ Average setup time reduced by 41% ✓ Amount of re-work reduced by 66%

Figure 22 Field Operations Setup Example

Issuance of Gear	
Problem to address: (from team charter)	Issuance of gear is chaotic, the space used is cluttered. X% of personnel receives incorrect sizes of gear.
Issues identified during project:	• Inventory unknown, can't verify • Rushed and last minute • Missing documentation • No standard, scheduled procedures
Root causes:	• No standard procedures or timeline • Unclear requirements and sizing • No standard locations or storage for gear • Personnel changeover between order and receipt (different sizes)

Recommendations:	✓ Documented procedures and space layout ✓ Training for new process ✓ Current personnel log with gear and sizing identified, updated during check-in process ✓ Inventory maintained and verified ✓ Standard timeline for ordering and issuance ✓ Distribution organized by kits
Results:	✓ Average time to issue reduced by X days ✓ Accuracy of issued gear sizes improved by 40%

Figure 23 Gear Issue Process Example

Procurement of Parts	
Problem to address: (from team charter)	Too much time is lost between when the need for a part is identified, and the order is actually placed. Too many authorizations are required to place an order.
Issues identified during project:	• Too many approvals required by internal policy • Priorities are incorrect or not adhered to • Trust and confidence in staff

	• Funds held by single person, causing bottleneck
Root causes:	• Senior staff has authority to approve purchase, but still must wait on finance signature • Unclear ownership of funds • Internal policy restrictions • Paper-based system, and signature authorities are located in different areas on the base
Recommendations:	✓ Designate single approval authority with visibility of funds ✓ Provide copies to finance to verify status of funds (no longer awaiting approval) ✓ Revised internal policy ✓ Electronic documentation ✓ Training for new process
Results:	✓ Reduced number of process steps from 57 to 9 ✓ Average process cycle time reduced by 90%

Figure 24 Parts Procurement Example

Many Things in Common ... We Already Knew That!

Looking through the examples above, we can all agree that they represent a variety of processes (remember, everything we do is a process). While the processes are different, did you see any commonalities across the project examples with respect to issues, root causes, recommendations, and results? There was a common thread of communication, training, varying procedures, missing information, unknowns, etc. that showed up several times. In the Lean Six Sigma world, practitioners see these things over and over again (it becomes fairly easy for the LSS expert to recognize certain patterns or problems, because they are so common!). Think of it this way: Joe works in process A. He knows it doesn't run as smoothly as it could, he has a few ideas for making the process better, but can't quite put his finger on the critical problem or solution. Sam is a LSS Black Belt who has facilitated over 30 teams in the past few years. He has grown to see common problems across varying processes. He can quickly help a team dial in to these common problems in the three basic areas of: cost, quality, and timeliness. Why is it so easy for Sam to see and a bit fuzzy for Joe? Well, why is it easy for a prize-winning chess player to see his opponent's strategy several steps ahead, or a musician to play a piece without a single mistake, or pro baseball player to recognize a pitch and respond accordingly? The answer is experience, and repetition. LSS facilitation is a skill that should improve and become sharpened over time and with experience. But, remember to watch out for arrogance. The best practitioners are humble about their knowledge and enjoy leading others toward discovery of their own solutions, rather than arriving as the know-it-all to save the day (even if they actually do know it all – they toss out guidance in bite-sized pieces so that the team can construct their own solutions – which helps to cultivate the skill and knowledge of team members).

Regarding recommendations and solutions, nearly every time I have been involved with a LSS project, the team outputs have included three basic things: a revised process, revised written procedures, and training for the new process or procedures. Usually other recommendations and improvements are made, too. But, the rebar-enforced concrete foundation of process improvement is the combination of process, procedures, and training.

At the conclusion of a project, in addition to all of the positive experiences and responses we have discussed, there may be a few knit brows. Often, with less complex processes, people voice opinions like "The solutions are so simple, we could have done this without Lean Six Sigma." Or "I knew this all along. We didn't need to spend a few weeks to figure this out." This feedback shouldn't be ignored. These sentiments are absolutely true! I take this opportunity to ask: "Why didn't you do this without Lean Six Sigma?" Sometimes I have found that LSS simply opens the door or creates the opportunity to do what everyone already knew needed to be done. Or possibly LSS grabs the attention of leadership, so the ideas of staff and personnel are finally heard. Looking into the past, it truly doesn't matter how long someone has had an idea. What matters is that the idea has blossomed into reality, and the process has improved. At that point, it is a win for the organization, the process owners, the project team, and those who are a daily part of the process, whether the solutions are surprisingly new, or even if they are nothing new at all.

Everything Has a Place: Everything in its Place (5S)

This section serves as a quick introduction to another Lean Six Sigma tool, known as "5S". So far, we have only discussed process improvements. What about cluttered and unmanageable spaces? We all know those people whose work spaces or houses are just a crazy mess. We wonder how they can possibly manage in that environment. Some messy people insist that they have a method that works for them. Maybe they do have a way of surviving amongst clutter, but I can assure you that no matter how much they argue with you, that environment is not conducive to efficient processes. If you have a messy warehouse, how do you know how much product you have on-hand, and when to re-order? If you have an out of control maintenance space, how do you quickly realize if oil is leaking or a tool is missing? If your house is a mess, how do you find that receipt when your laptop dies during the warranty period? For that matter, how do you clean? Yuck!

I tell people that a 5S world would be my utopia. I am much more at peace in a neat and tidy environment. This tendency is common among Lean Sig Sigma practitioners, and as long as the "neat and straight" fever (illness?) stays at a reasonable temperature, this tendency can be quite helpful.

When describing 5S to students or teams, I like to tell a story about my neighbor with a 5S garage. I'm always delighted when his garage door is open and I get a chance to peak in (in a non-stalker way, of course) as I pass by. The floor has black and white checkerboard tiles, the cabinets all match. He has peg-board walls and even tool outlines on some of the boards. I just want to step inside and bask in the glory of that organized garage. Zen, I tell you!

So, what is 5S? You know 5S, without even reading the full description. Your second-grade teacher practiced it in the classroom; there are stores and experts who make lots of money supporting 5S approaches; hospitals, manufacturers, businesses, every possible industry has been using 5S principles since well before we called it 5S. The "5S" tool is an off-shoot from Lean Six Sigma. It was first defined by the Japanese automotive industry[24], and fits nicely alongside the

---

[24] 5S has roots in Japanese auto manufacturing, around the time of Deming and Ishikawa. The original version of 5S: Seiri, Seiton, Seiso, Seiketsu, and Shitsuke.

process concepts of Lean Six Sigma. 5S is quite a nifty approach to layout and space improvement. The five-step approach is summarized by five words, all beginning with the letter S. Incredibly unexpected, I know, given the name. Let's take a look at these fantastic S-words:

- 1. SORT: Once the space has been identified (it may be a closet, a warehouse, a manufacturing floor, my garage…), everything in that space must be categorized in one of three categories:

    o Keep: It is used often enough that it should be kept in the area.

    o Store: It is used, but not as often, so can be stored somewhere else.

    o Toss: It is not needed, get rid of it.

    At this point, I should mention that there are many variations of this. If you watch the shows on home improvement cable channels, such as "Clean My House" or "I'm a Slob" (there aren't really shows with these names, but you know what I mean), you may have seen that their three categories are: Keep, Sell, Throw Away. Nearly the same thing. Use whatever categories work for your situation.

- 2. SIMPLIFY: (This step is sometimes called STRAIGHTEN.) Establish a standard location for all of the items in the "Keep" pile. Also, make sure you know where you sent the occasionally needed items from the "Store" pile.

    This is a great time for the imagination to engage: labels, colored tape outlines, maps, foam cut-outs, peg boards with outlines, standard toolboxes… the world is your oyster. Be creative, or invite a neat freak to the party for some help. When you are finished, there should be a place for everything, and everything should be in its place. And it should pass the "sniff test": ask a visitor to stop by and get his or her reactions. The descriptive words from the visitor should be in the general vicinity of neat, tidy, clean, etc.

At this point, if your 5S space is a part of a larger space, the excluded people will begin to notice the change. I visited an outdoor maintenance bay at a military base a few years ago. The person in charge was all too happy to give me a quick tour and brag on his team who made the improvements (this is common, by the way, people are happy and proud to show their 5S results). He described the improvements and then told me about others who worked nearby and saw the results, and then opted to 5S their spaces. Before long, the supply space that supported the maintenance bays also underwent a 5S transformation. 5S is like that little sprig of peppermint I planted in my back yard a few years ago. It has spread like crazy, and it smells good, too.

- 3. SYSTEMATIC CLEANING: (This step is sometimes called SWEEP or SHINE.) Keep it clean, and orderly. All day and every day. Don't wait for the cleaning lady to show up every other Tuesday. This is everyone's responsibility. In a more formal 5S program, the cleaning responsibilities may be documented to include space assignments, methods, tools, supplies, and frequencies.

This is where my zen garage fails. I live with three people who don't share the same love for all things organized. When I 5S the family garage, I typically make it to 2S, go off course in the third S, have dreams of fourth and fifth S, but never quite reach the dream. There is an obvious crack in my 5S foundation. It's the word "I". The rest of the family unit doesn't feel the need to systematically clean because they didn't get down and dirty with the first two S's. No skin in the game. They weren't out there with the dirt and cobwebs. They didn't feel the satisfaction of transforming the mess into order. The same will happen in your environment if you opt to take a weekend to 5S your working space. By excusing the team from the work, you are giving them permission to be excused from the upkeep; you are making it less important to them, and possibly the worst thing is that they have been robbed of the feelings of accomplishment, pride, and team cohesiveness that they could have experienced. I know it's sometimes easier to do it on your own (trust me, I am the queen of doing it on my own because it is quicker and easier). But, in the long run, it is best to involve the team in the 5S endeavor.

- 4. STANDARDIZE: Document the new space and procedures. Train everyone on the new layout and procedures. When I recently supported a 5S project for a supply area, the team created a map of the space, written procedures for keeping the space orderly and for replenishing supplies, and a training plan for existing and incoming personnel. By completing the 5S, this smaller unit was able to cut supply expense in half, saving $5,000 per month. That may not seem like a lot, but if the results are sustained, this represents a permanent savings, which adds up to $60,000 in a year, or $300,000 over five years. The savings become significant over time.

- 5. SUSTAIN: (This step is sometimes called SELF DISCIPLINE.) Keep up the good work. Report status on a regular basis. Train new employees on the standard procedures. Establish a 5S audit program. Review the space for further improvements.

   The first three S's are about transforming a disorganized space into an organized space. The final two S's are about keeping it that way. Maintenance can be the hardest part! We are all human, and know that it's easy to let things slowly disintegrate. Sometimes we even go back to the original conditions, not because they were better, but because they are familiar. There are probably many psychological studies on this, well out of my realm of expertise. I'm just making general observations of things that are strange, but so true.

- SAFETY: This is the bonus S. Some organizations call their program "6S" rather than 5S. This provides an added emphasis on Safety. There is nothing wrong with tailoring any of these tools for an added emphasis on anything that is particularly important to your organization.

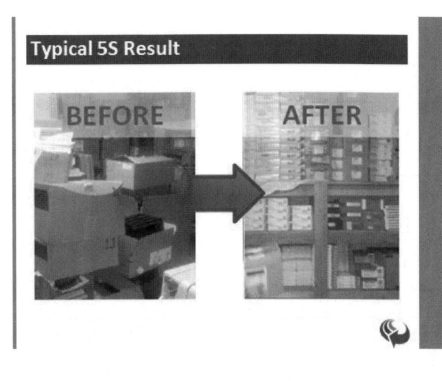

Figure 25 Typical 5S Result

Pictures

We've all grown up with the saying: A picture is worth a thousand words. I must disagree. There are no words that can replace a picture in Lean Six Sigma. Pictures are invaluable in our world of process improvement. I once worked with a warehouse team, and arrived after the initial 5S activities. The warehouse could only be described as a piece of heaven, complete with the skies opening up and angels singing. It was spotless, organized, perfect. I have honestly never seen a better 5S result. But, guess what was missing... the "before" pictures. Several people told me horror stories of what the spaces looked like beforehand, how difficult it was to perform daily duties, the dangers associated with the mess, even an event when a fork-lift nearly overturned due to the old setup. But, there were no pictures. What a shame.

Luckily, we live in an age when nearly everyone who practices Lean Six Sigma has a camera at hand, in a cell phone or tablet, usually in their pocket or purse. Get in the habit of using your camera. The joke in my family is that I have more pictures of work (team meetings, processes, classes) than of my own family. It is now part of my routine to ALWAYS take pictures at the conclusion of every team meeting of all items on the walls (remember, we use chart paper and butcher paper along with markers and sticky notes so that all meeting activities are visible to everyone in the room), I take pictures during each day of class to show progress throughout the week, I take pictures on site visits to represent what is really going on and to have a reference for later discussions. I even take pictures when I am in someone else's meeting – this is due to a personal experience: Once, I sat in on a meeting where the facilitator was using a white board (which is perfectly fine, in place of paper, if available), as I had done many times before. But, two weeks after this particularly productive meeting, I was called by the team leader with panic in his voice. He asked if I had taken pictures of the white board. I had not. No one had, and of course, the board had been erased by mistake. There were two problems with this situation: (1) no pictures had been taken; and (2) the project file or project documents had not been updated immediately following the meeting (I like to update the project file within twenty-four hours, if possible), so the white board was still the only source of the critical team information. After that incident, I decided that as long as I asked permission, it might be better to take pictures of all meetings that I attend, rather than not be able to help in a future team documentation emergency! This has further compounded the joke that I have more pictures of work than my family.

I can't emphasize enough: TAKE PICTURES! Not only do pictures serve as critical visible information (for example, before and after pictures), they save a great deal of time. The streamlined approach that I use, with all team tools documented in a single project file, includes many pictures from meetings. For instance, I do not take the time to type up the SIPOC after the team conducts that exercise, or the "As-Is" process, or even the fishbone diagrams. These particular tools serve their purpose during the team activity itself. The knowledge gained by conducting these activities is what we seek. We will not train staff to the old process, or SIPOC, or fishbone diagram. They will not be attachments to a future operational procedure document. So, there is no need to take the time to type them up, AS LONG AS YOU HAVE A PICTURE. You do need to document team tools and activities. But, in many cases, a picture will do. I simply drop the actual picture into my project file, and move on to the next tool. This is a big time saver. And, I think people appreciate seeing the real thing, an actual picture, on occasion.

Summary

It is a good idea to sit back and ponder your 5S (or DMAIC) plans. Picture how your organization, the environment, the politics, the personalities, the strengths and weaknesses will all be affected by process improvement. I can pretty much guarantee that the reality won't match what you imagine. But, this is a great exercise to address areas that may need tailoring, emphasis, or even some reconnaissance to better understand current conditions.

When starting out in the Lean Six Sigma world, as a facilitator, if you plan to do it well, make sure to schedule time for thought and scenario planning. Trust me, this will not be a waste of time. Practice the tools, actually go through a dress rehearsal of sorts with paper on a wall, and pretend you are running the meeting. Get to know the art and science associated with the tools. Settle on the level of detail that is best for your process map, how you will determine the items for which to conduct root cause analyses, how you will manage a particularly talkative team member... the options for planning are immense. Perhaps, when starting out, an hour of planning for each team meeting is reasonable. As time goes by, you will settle in to the right amount of planning resulting in a smoothly run team meeting.

The most important thing to remember is that you are not alone. There is always someone with more experience who can help: a colleague, friend, consultant, or the guy you met at the last ASQ chapter meeting[25]. There is always someone. Let them help you grow. Let them help you avoid common pitfalls.

---

[25] Further information for the American Society for Quality can be found at: www.asq.org.

PART 5. FINAL NOTES

– Do what you love, love what you do, and don't forget to take pictures!

You Have Been Given a Golden Ticket

By reading this book, and jumping into the world of Lean Six Sigma, you have been given a Golden Ticket. Such life changing information is rare. The Lean Six Sigma tools and skill set can be used anywhere, anytime, by anyone. The tools we give to our Marines in our Lean Six Sigma program can be used for the rest of their lives, anywhere they go.

If you are a seasoned Lean Six Sigma practitioner, I hope that the conversation in this book has provided another perspective and options for consideration as you support others. Lean Six Sigma doesn't need to be complex, and we don't need to bring the fanciest tools to the table when a simple one will do.

If you are just starting out, or thought that this thin book on the topic might be a quicker read than some of the thicker ones in print, my hope is that you will have an itch to learn more. As I stated at the beginning of this book, this approach can be used to benefit your life, the lives of others, and particularly those of your loved ones. When you help people help themselves to become more productive, better aligned with their organizations, participants in change, and more satisfied with life, it comes around full-circle. You've helped yourself experience these things, and you become a better family member, you create career and financial opportunities, personal satisfaction increases, which all contribute to your pursuit of happiness and overall joy.

If You Aren't Going to Finish, It's Better Not to Start

Let's put some realism in the middle of all of this happy-joy talk. I truly believe all that we have been discussing. The majority of Lean Six Sigma can be life-changing and good. But I'd like to offer a word of warning: if you aren't going to finish, then don't start. To clarify, sometimes projects hit delays or shift. Sometimes the team recommendations aren't the best fit, and alternatives are found. That's not what I am talking about here. This discussion is primarily for LEADERS in the organization: Lean Six Sigma is not a flavor of the month. For many organizations, this will be the first time that employees are truly asked to engage in determining the direction of the organization and improving their own processes. It is a new freedom that creates a new atmosphere. If leadership engages a team in Lean Six Sigma, and then doesn't take their recommendations seriously, or directs a group to be trained, but doesn't let them use their new skills, then the employee satisfaction levels may end up being worse than if Lean Six Sigma had not been introduced at all. There's nothing wrong with trial projects to prove the concept, or keeping the program small. That's a perfectly logical approach. After all, I can understand the person who slowly inches into the pool rather than jumping right in (I am one of those people, too). But, to give people a taste of this amazing toolset and then remove it is almost cruel. Don't do it.

Lessons Learned

This entire book can be viewed as lessons I have learned while supporting Lean Six Sigma in the Marine Corps. Here is a super-quick review of highlights:

- As you gain experience over time, you will be able to see common patterns and problems across varying processes. This is good. It is normal. But, don't let it blind you to other important signs that you should see. It's easy to get comfortable with what is familiar, but continue to challenge yourself to see beyond what you know.

Lean to the Corps

- Standard tools are a must. Find the best way to package and manage your tools and templates. Don't waste time creating or re-creating in any facet of Lean Six Sigma (briefs, emails, folders, forms, training material, etc.). Build your arsenal, whatever works best for you. Don't let another experienced practitioner convince (or even bully sometimes!) you to use something that doesn't make sense to you.

- Find your comfort zone, and then push a little further. Once you begin to collect and build your tools and contacts, working in one industry or another, own it. Become the best expert you can. Then look to expand. If you start out in the manufacturing world, it may be exciting to expand to medical, or construction, or anything else. If you are in the public sector, perhaps the private sector can provide a new challenge. If you are certified as a Lean Six Sigma Black Belt, then go for Master Black Belt. Seek certifications in supporting skills such as 5S or Theory of Constraints.

- Don't over-regulate yourself or others. Keep an open mind. What works best for you, may not be best for others. If your organization standardizes approaches or documents, make sure they are adding value and not preventing growth. A great idea for structuring your Lean Six Sigma may not meet all of your organization's needs, so try to allow for a combination of approaches (such as top-down and bottom-up identification of projects, described in Part 3 of this book).

- Celebrate successes. Lean Six Sigma results in measurable improvements. Once you have this documented, celebrate! Tell others, announce it over the loud speakers, plaster it on the company web-site, in the newsletter, at the annual conference. Make sure that people know about the good things that are happening, and who is doing them. If you have money for bonuses, use it. But if not, don't worry. Celebrating doesn't need to cost a lot. I know of a command that passes a sledgehammer that has been painted red to the most recently successful team. The team is awarded the sledgehammer during formation (a meeting with everyone present). The team representative is allowed to use the sledgehammer to demolish an item of choice (such as pumpkin) during formation. It's silly, it's fun, and it costs very little. It also highlights a group of people for their Lean Six Sigma success, and is a morale booster. Options for celebration are endless.

- Keep a repository or library of projects. For projects to really make an impact, they need to be visible to others. Posters on walls that show project summaries, particularly near the boss's office, in the lobby, or in a common area, can provide such visibility. But, when a new team is formed, and wants to see what other process improvements have taken place, they will need a repository. When the heads of the organization get together to review successes for the year, they will need a repository. When your organization benchmarks with another organization, yes, they will need the repository, too. There are many web-based tools that can serve this function. Or, shared folders on an intranet can serve this rudimentary purpose. In my experience, the most useful aspects of the repository or library are:
  - o Single location for documenting all organization projects
  - o Key word search to find projects of similar nature
  - o Points of contact listed for each project
  - o Trained people identified by level of training (Green Belt, Black Belt, etc.)
  - o Single location to house templates and training materials
  - o Visibility of projects organized by individuals or participants (this can serve as a facilitator's project portfolio)
  - o Opportunity (for more mature programs) to roll up and report results
- Don't forget to replicate. If you improve a local process, there are most likely people in the organization conducting the same or similar processes elsewhere. Replicate your improvements by sharing and standardizing across the board. This may be difficult with varying middle-management, but if the top boss is on-board, then he or she can direct everyone to engage and participate in replication. If the top boss is not on-board, then this should be seen as an opportunity for you to tell the story

of Lean Six Sigma, using concrete results and your power of persuasion to build a swell of support.

Personal Advice

Lean Six Sigma can have a real and lasting influence on the lives of those who practice it. Treat your experience and education like a marathon. It is a long-term commitment. At times you may run, and at other times walk. As long as you are moving forward, you are benefiting. As one project wraps up, make sure to look for another. If your organization engages in Lean Six Sigma, find professional communities or training opportunities to support the effort. If you are growing your own skills, build relationships with others in the field, take a class at the local University, teach a class, mentor a colleague, establish your own consulting business. Your options are limited only by your imagination.

Reading over this basic advice, I realize that it applies not only to Lean Six Sigma, but anything deemed worthwhile in life. I will end with these simple recommendations: Challenge yourself. Do what you love. And love what you do.

Recommended Reading

Collins, Jim. *Good to Great*. New York: HarperCollins, 2001. Print.

George, Michael L., et al. *Lean Six Sigma Pocket Toolbook*. New York: McGraw-Hill, 2005. Print.

Frigon, Normand and Harry Jackson. *Enterprise Excellence*. Hoboken, New Jersey: John Wiley & Sons, Inc., 2009. Print.

Krulak, Victor. *First to Fight*. Annapolis, MD: First Bluejacket Books, 1999. Print.

Goldratt, Eliyahu M.. *The Goal*. Great Barrington, MA: The North River Press, 1984. Print.

Lencioni, Patrick. *Three Signs of a Miserable Job*. San Francisco, CA: Jossey-Bass, 2007. Print.

George, Mike, Dave Rowlands, and Bill Kastle. *What is Lean Six Sigma?*. New York: McGraw-Hill, 2004. Print.

Slater, Robert. *The GE Way Fieldbook*. New York: McGraw-Hill, 2000. Print.

Slater, Robert. *The GE Way*. New York: McGraw-Hill, 1999. Print.

INDEX

Lean to the Corps

Made in the USA
Columbia, SC
04 August 2019